NEW VANGUARD 233

VALENTINE INFANTRY TANK 1938–45

BRUCE OLIVER NEWSOME Ph.D   ILLUSTRATED BY H. MORSHEAD

First published in Great Britain in 2016 by Osprey Publishing,
PO Box 883, Oxford, OX1 9PL, UK
PO Box 3985, New York, NY 10185-3985, USA
E-mail: info@ospreypublishing.com

Osprey Publishing, part of Bloomsbury Publishing Plc

A CIP catalogue record for this book is available from the British Library

Print ISBN: 978 1 4728 1375 6
 PDF ebook ISBN: 978 1 4728 1376 3
 ePub ebook ISBN: 978 1 4728 1377 0

Index by Rob Munro
Typeset in Sabon and Myriad Pro
Originated by PDQ Media, Bungay, UK
Printed in China through World Print Ltd

16 17 18 19 20   10 9 8 7 6 5 4 3 2 1

www.ospreypublishing.com

ACKNOWLEDGEMENTS

The author thanks David Willey (Curator), David Fletcher (Historian), Stuart Wheeler (Archive and Library Manager), and Katie Thompson (Archive Assistant) for assistance with the archives and collections at The Tank Museum in Bovington, England.

The author thanks B. John Pearson, Colin Pearson, Jack Pearson and Jennifer D. Catlin for mechanical and operational assistance with surviving Valentine tanks.

The author also thanks B. John Pearson for prior research on the production of Valentines, Harold Skaarup for information on Canadian Valentines, and Leland Ness for prior research on British and Canadian exports.

Cover photo by Fox Photos/Getty Images.

All other photographs are courtesy of The Tank Museum.

CONTENTS

VALENTINE INFANTRY TANK 1938–45

INTRODUCTION

More tanks and their derivatives were produced during World War II on the Valentine tank platform than on any other British tank platform. Valentines and Valentine derivatives accounted for about 25 per cent of all the tank platforms produced in Britain during the war, about 25 per cent of those produced in Canada, and almost 75 per cent of the tanks exported by Britain and Canada to the Soviet Union. Valentines saw service across North Africa and Italy, through France to Germany, from India to Burma, from New Zealand to Guadalcanal, and from Russia to Berlin.

Yet the design started out in 1938 as a stop-gap infantry tank, with inferior specifications to the Infantry Tank Mark II (Matilda II), on the promise of quicker, cheaper production, and more reliable automotive performance, which it certainly achieved.

A Valentine I and Matilda II have been loaded on the same Warflat wagon, indicating the Valentine I's lower profile and simpler production, but inferior protection and cramped interior.

DESIGN AND DEVELOPMENT

From A10 to Valentine

In April 1937, Vulcan Foundry refused the Mechanization Board's invitation to develop a new medium tank until it had completed the Matilda II. On

10 February 1938 the War Office, desperate for more medium tanks, invited Vickers to develop a derivative of the Matilda II or the Vickers A10 (Cruiser II). Vickers naturally chose to develop the A10. Vickers judged the capacity of the A10 platform at 16 long tons (17.92 short tons; 16.26 metric tons), which would limit the armour standard to 60mm – the minimum specification – and limit the turret crew to two, when the specification was for three. Vickers suggested a Vickers 40mm cannon in place of the Royal Ordnance 40mm 2-pounder gun, to allow an even smaller turret.

The second meeting occurred the day before Valentine's Day, 14 February 1938. 'Valentine' was also the middle name of Sir John Carden, who had led the design of the A9 and A10, although he had died before the Valentine was designed. 'Valentine' was also an acronym of the supplier (Vickers Armstrong Limited (Engineers), Newcastle-upon-Tyne).

The project aimed at a stop-gap Infantry Tank Mark III. As inducements, Vickers promised that the automotive line would need no development, and promised production from March 1939. Vickers also estimated a cost of about two-thirds of the Matilda's (although the price of production in the first contract of 1939 would be about nine-tenths). Accepting these promises, the War Office agreed to a mock-up tank with a 50mm basis and a Vickers 2-pounder.

However, when the mock-up was shown on 24 March 1938 to user and mechanization authorities they rejected the thin armour and the inadequate vision for the commander (limited to a single periscope). For a while the project was dormant, although the Superintendent of Design was working on a mounting to a 75mm armour standard.

In April 1939, after more delays to the Matilda II, the War Office invited Vickers back. Vickers offered a four-man 50mm turret or a two-man 60mm turret. The General Staff settled on the latter. Vickers estimated full production from April 1940, at four tanks per month. The Director of Staff Duties (DSD) doubted whether such a low rate of production justified such a design. He noted that the A10's running gear was vulnerable to wire, and asked whether skirting plates could be added. Vickers claimed that the platform could not afford the extra weight of skirting plates unless ammunition were reduced, and estimated that 3mm-thick plates would weigh not more than 0.2 long

This Valentine I is at Lulworth in Dorset, after completion of gunnery trials. Its Bren machine-gun is in the sprung, angle-poised 'Lakeman' mounting.

BELOW LEFT
This Bren (without magazine) is being demonstrated on the 'Lakeman' mounting by 'A' Squadron, 2nd Lothian & Border Horse, 6th Armoured Division, in September 1942.

BELOW RIGHT
This Valentine I illustrates the wide internal mantlet common to the Valentine I, II, IV, VI and VII. This tank has the first design of track, which was lightest but least durable. The malleable cast iron shoes were materially softer than steel shoes, and the double pin link suffered more stress than a single pin link.

Valentine Mark	Infantry Tank Mark	Deliveries (excl. conversions)	Evolutionary basis	External differentiation		Turret front	Turret sides
				Main armament	Coaxial machine-gun		
I	III	308	A10 (Cruiser II)	40mm 2-pounder gun, without muzzle brake or counter weight	7.92mm Besa on right of main armament	internal mantlet, behind a wide rectangular curved opening	On right side: square revolver port. On left side: either no port (tanks T15946 to T16555 and T20419 to T20493); or a D-shaped port (mostly Valentine IIs)
II	III*	1,511	Valentine I plus AEC diesel engine				
III (New Zealand converted 18 to III CS)	-	536	Valentine II plus 3-man turret	40mm 2-pounder gun (III CS had 76mm howitzer), without muzzle brake or counter weight		Internal mantlet, behind an almost square flat mounting; narrow elliptical casting at base of main gun	Circular revolver ports on both sides
IV	III**	524	Valentine I plus GMC engine	40mm 2-pounder gun, without muzzle brake or counter weight		As Valentine I/II	As Valentine I/II
V	-	1,208 (including 212 DDs)	Valentine IV hull, Valentine III turret			As Valentine III	As Valentine V
VI	III***	30	Valentine IV adapted to Canadian capacity		7.92mm Besa; 7.62mm Browning from sixteenth vehicle on	As Valentine I/II, except after first 100 vehicles the rivets were eliminated, although still bolted around the top and bottom	As Valentine I/II, except D-shaped port added after first 100 vehicles
VII	III***	1,390	Valentine VI adapted to Number 19 radio		7.62mm Browning		
VIIA	-		Valentine IV with changes to exterior and engine compartment				
VIII	-	0	Valentine III plus 57mm gun	57mm 6-pounder gun, with counter-weight on muzzle (Mark III was shorter than Mark V)	None	External mantlet	Circular revolver ports on both sides; backwards-sloped bracket for two 4-inch smoke projectors on right side
IX	-	1,323 (including 236 DDs)	Valentine V plus Valentine VIII's turret			External mantlet; Mounting Number 1 Mark 1	
X	-	135	Valentine IX with Besa machine-gun		7.92mm Besa in protruding box on right of main armament	External mantlet; Mounting Number 4 Mark 1	
XI	-	295 (including 175 DDs)	Valentine X with 75mm gun	75mm gun with muzzle brake (1 hole each side)		External mantlet; Mounting Number 1 Mark 5	
Heavy Valentine (Valiant)	-	1 pilot	Valentine IX's automotive line, with independent concentric coil/wishbone suspension and thicker armour	75mm gun, without muzzle brake, until added after war	7.92mm Besa mounted internally to left of main armament	Internal mantlet within curved casting; on each side, a column of 5 large bolts affixed the front casting to turret sides	Semi-elliptical casting without apertures
Heavy Valiant	-	0	Valiant with thicker armour and same running gear as US T1/M6 heavy tank and British Heavy Cromwell	57mm gun, 75mm gun, or 95mm howitzer			
Bishop	-	1 pilot and 149 production vehicles	Valentine III hull with tall fixed superstructure for a 25-pounder gun	87.6 mm 25-pounder gun/howitzer; no muzzle brake; box-shaped cradle extending partway under barrel	None	External mantlet; protruding gun cradle; tall narrow vertical mounting; upper plate slopes backwards towards roof	Tall vertical sides, each welded to front plate; roof is bolted to internal angle plates
Archer	-	2 pilots and 665 production vehicles	Valentine V hull with new superstructure and mounting for 17-pounder gun	76mm 17-pounder Mark II gun with muzzle brake (2 holes each side)		No turret; superstructure extended at hull front	No turret; superstructure extended from hull sides

tons. DSD agreed to a reduction of ammunition to 50 rounds in order to add skirting plates and Vickers guaranteed a speed of 15 miles per hour (mph).

The meeting discussed also an attachment to carry a plough, which would be raised and lowered hydraulically through a power take-off from the gearbox, but Vickers opposed this attachment. The meeting agreed that it could be omitted only from training vehicles.

| Valentine Mark | External differentiation | | Internal differentiation | | |
	Turret rear	Hull	Crewmen in fighting compartment	Radio	Engine compartment
I	Armoured cover hanging down over the air exfiltration slit: earlier design ended with a straight edge (T15946 to T16013, T16221 to 16233, T16356 to T16378, T16381, T16390, T16393, T20419 to T20423, T20427, T20430 to T20432); most covers had a curved lip; Army workshops would add bracketed boxes on each corner (each for 2 Bren magazines)	All riveted and bolted; 100 Valentine Is (T15946 to T16045) had hinges and handles on only the nearside rear access door, and a fuel tank filler under a flap towards the offside; 75 Valentine Is (T16046 to T16120) had hinges and handles on both doors, and fuel filler on inside	2	Number 11 low power with 6-foot rod aerial	AEC spark-ignition engine, with fuel tanks either side, Meadows gearbox
II		As final Valentine Is; Desert Service vehicles had sandguards, auxiliary fuel tank on left trackguard, and container for 5 water cans below the access door		Number 11 or Number 19	AEC diesel engine with fuel tank on nearside, Meadows gearbox
III (New Zealand converted 18 to III CS)	Commander's rotating hatch set towards rear; bulge slopes backward and downward towards straight edge; one large box for Bren magazines bracketed centrally and horizontally.		3	Number 19	
IV	As Valentine I/II, except all had curved exfiltration cover		2		GMC 6.71S diesel, Spicer gearbox
V	As Valentine III		3		
VI	As Valentine IV, except first vehicle had straight exfiltration cover	As Valentine I/II, except cast nose after first 100 vehicles; otherwise riveted and bolted; splash angles in front of turret ring	2	Number 11	
VII				Number 19	
VIIA		As above, with: protective cages over headlamps; convoy lamp; ice-studs on tracks; auxiliary fuel tank			As above, except: extra engine oil cooler; batteries moved to rear
VIII	As Valentine III, except box is bracketed at a slope; Vickers welded all these tanks, but Metropolitan Cammell welded only the last Valentine Xis	as Valentine III			AEC diesel
IX		as Valentine V			540 vehicles had GMC 6.71S; 783 vehicles had GMC 6.71A
X		as Valentine IX, except: mostly welded, some rivets; protective cages over headlamps; splash angles in front of turret ring			GMC 6.71A diesel
XI		as Valentine X, except cast nose			
Heavy Valentine (Valiant)	Large cast bin, welded to rear	Cast and welded front with concave driver's plate; trackguards but no side skirts; 6 evenly spaced wheels, each with vertical springs	2		GMC 6.71M diesel, governed at higher speed and power than in Archer
Heavy Valiant		Side skirts; 3 evenly spaced bogies, each with 2 parallel pairs of wheels, and horizontal volute springs (HVSS)			Rolls-Royce Meteorite
Bishop	vertically split doors opening outwards; the container carrying five water cans was affixed to the lefthand door, but sometimes relocated to a trackguard	As Valentine III	3	Number 18 Mark III, gradually replaced in field by Number 19	AEC diesel, Meadows gearbox
Archer	No turret; gun mounted rearwards over engine compartment	Hull superstructure extended at front and sides, all welded	3		GMC 6.71M diesel

The DSD kept wondering out loud why Vickers could not produce the Matilda II, which was fully developed and more capable, but Vickers claimed that it could produce two of its design to one Matilda II. News of delays in the supply of armour for the Matilda II was the final justification for an agreement to order 100 tanks as soon as Vickers could assure fulfilment of the General Staff minimum specifications, which it did on 4 April.

The Director of Mechanization (Major-General Alexander Davidson) had been decisive in warning of the Matilda II's risks. On 4 April, he promised that the War Office would almost certainly order 200–250 Valentines, following Treasury approval, of which Vickers should produce 50, with deliveries from May or June 1940, while other contractors would assemble the rest. On 9 April, the General Staff settled on 300 Valentines. On 15 May, Vickers was put on notice to produce 50 tanks, while Metro-Cammell and Birmingham Railway Carriage & Wagon Company (BRCWC) were put on notice to make 125 each. In July 1939, an order was placed with Vickers alone for 275 vehicles to be delivered in May 1940. No pilot vehicles were ordered.

This is one of the first 50 Valentine Is out of Vickers, with the slightly heavier and more durable steel shoes (still with double pin links). It is being followed by a Matilda II on a cross-country course in Northern Command.

This Valentine II illustrates the distinctive engine compartment of all Valentines: air was taken in over the engine and expelled by fans through the sloping rear. The armour covering the air exfiltration slit at the rear of the turret has a curved lip; earlier covers had a straight lip.

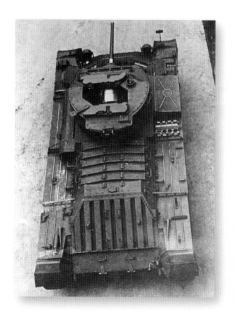

By September 1939, the skirting plates had been dropped. Instead, the Ministry of Supply asked if a fender bar could be incorporated to mitigate the chance of wire becoming entangled in the tracks. Also in September the Fowler plough attachment was deleted.

New engines and gearboxes

The Valentine Mark I (Valentine I), as delivered from May 1940, had a spark-ignition engine (A189) by AEC. The Valentine II had the slightly less powerful but more economical diesel version (A190). Both had a 5-speed clash-type gearbox by Meadows.

AEC was already an unreliable supplier, so, early in 1940, the Directorate of Mechanization (in July 1940 this became the Department of Tank Design or DTD) tried a diesel engine of the same capacity by General Motors Corporation (GMC). AEC carried out the trials under DTD's supervision. The Valentine IV was a Valentine II adapted for the GMC engine and a gearbox by Spicer (another American company). The Spicer gearbox had clash gears in first and fifth, and syncromesh gears in second, third and fourth gears.

All 308 Valentine Is received the A189 spark-ignition engine. All Valentine IIs, Valentine IIIs, and Bishops had the AEC A190 diesel engine. All Valentine IVs, Valentine Vs, Valentine VIs, Valentine VIIs, and 540 of the 1,323 Valentine IXs received the GMC 6.71S engine (the 'S' type of the Type 6004 engine). The remaining 783 Valentine IXs, all Valentine Xs, and all Valentine XIs received the more powerful 'A' type (thanks to larger fuel injectors and a higher governed speed). The Archers (self-propelled 17-pounder guns) received the more powerful 6.71M, which was uprated further for the Valiant tank.

Canadian versions

In early September 1940, a British detachment landed in Canada with a Valentine I and a Matilda II, which shortly travelled to the US, while the Valentine stayed at Camp Borden with part of the detachment.

The British Ministry of Supply's tank mission ordered the Angus Works of the Canadian Pacific Railway Company (a subsidiary in Montreal of American Locomotive) to assemble 300 Valentine hulls. The British mission ordered British-designed armaments and ammunition from suppliers on the other side of the St Lawrence River, but sourced the GMC engine, the Spicer gearbox and suspension arms from America. The British at home redesigned the Valentine II as the Valentine IV to accommodate the American-sourced sub-assemblies. Late in 1940, they despatched a pilot Valentine IV with drawings, which the Canadians redrew for metric units and locally sourced armour. L.E. 'Ted' Carr was despatched from the British Tank Mission in the US to help, resulting in a cast nose after the first 100 vehicles. The Canadian version was designated as Valentine VI, until the turret was redesigned slightly to accept a Number 19 wireless set, producing the Valentine VII. The Valentine VIIa was adapted slightly for Soviet use.

Upgunned Valentines and self-propelled guns

In September 1941, the General Staff declared the Valentine obsolete, and urgently required a replacement. In the meantime, they urged rearmament with the 6-pounder gun as a stop-gap. However, in December 1941, the Ministry of Supply reported that the tank's turret did not offer room for a larger gun, and was working out how to mount a 6-pounder on a turretless platform as a self-propelled gun (SP or SPG).

On 4 June 1942, Vickers (of Chertsey) sent a self-propelled 6-pounder gun on a Valentine I hull for automotive trials, but after just 76 miles it was sent back on 6 June without further interest. Around then, the Ministry authorized a Valentine with a 6-pounder in a turret. DTD's design accommodated the 6-pounder gun, but only two crewmen and no coaxial machine-gun. The prospect of this turret and the Valentine II/III hull was known as Valentine VIII, but the Valentine V hull was substituted in order to standardize the GMC engine, except that the side armour was reduced further. This combination was the Valentine IX, which was delivered from late 1942 to mid-1943.

The Valentine X, which was delivered from July 1943, benefited from a coaxial machine-gun. The Valentine XI, which was delivered from February 1944, had a 75mm gun.

The Valentines IX, X and XI were the first British tanks to be assembled with armoured ammunition bins, although each successive mark lost stowage in favour of guns.

The Valiant (A38)

On 7 May 1942, the Tank Board had approved development of an assault tank (eventually the A33 or Heavy Cromwell), but its basis – the Cruiser VIII – was still developmental.

On 26 June 1942, Vickers formally proposed an 'assault tank', to be developed from the Valentine, with thicker armour and a 6-pounder gun, at 23 long tons altogether (25.76 short tons; 23.37 metric tons), and without growing wider than the railway loading gauge. In the proposal, Vickers emphasized the low risk of an unambitious development with existing components, as it had emphasized in 1938 when marketing the Valentine tank. Vickers anticipated a pilot vehicle in 12 months.

The outline drawings and wooden model looked like the Valentine X, except for a door in the left turret side for the gunner, a single split hatch in the turret roof, a glacis sloping backwards and left and right from the longitudinal centre line, independently sprung larger roadwheels, and a wider track.

In August 1942, the Ministry of Supply contracted with Vickers for three pilot tanks in mild steel, shortly amended to six: four Valiant Is were to be fitted with either the GMC or the AEC diesel engine; two Valiant IIs were to be fitted with prospective V8 engines by either Ford or Rolls-Royce.

On 25 September 1942, Vickers proposed that 'the initial batch of production vehicles' (Valiant I, the same as specified in June)

This Valentine I is towing a Cruiser IVa during recovery trials in late 1940.

In December 1941, the Director of Artillery suggested a 6-pounder gun in a partial turret on the rear of a Valentine; the engine compartment would be relocated forwards. Instead, Vickers (at Chertsey) took a 6-pounder gun off its towed carriage, and placed it atop a fabricated pedestal affixed to the top of the driver's compartment of a Valentine I. Pivoting in this pedestal, the gun has been traversed to face the photographer. To shield the crew, plates were affixed vertically, by means of angle plates, to the trackguard and along the forward edge of the engine compartment. The central of the three plates at the rear was hinged as a door. The shields were not completed on the offside for this photograph, although presumably the vehicle was complete for its only known demonstration, at Farnborough, from 4 to 6 June 1942.

The Valentine IX had a 6-pounder gun but no machine-gun or 2-inch smoke projector to its offside. Instead, a bracket was affixed on the side of the turret for two 4-inch projectors.

should be powered by a GMC engine uprated to 210 brake horse power (bhp), while a Valiant II would be developed with an engine developing 400 to 500bhp (presumably the Rolls-Royce Meteorite) and an adjusted transmission.

On 22 October 1942, the Ministry of Supply placed an order with Vickers for 500 Valiants, but soon cancelled it. In January 1943, the Ministry transferred the automotive part of the project to Rolls-Royce's engine facility at Belper, then under contract with the Ministry of Supply. W.A. Robotham was head of research at Rolls-Royce, and since November 1941 also Chief Engineer Tank Design at the Ministry of Supply, at which point Belper had become a contracted research and development facility. Nobody there had ever designed a tank until Belper started designing the Heavy Cromwell in September 1941, but Robotham's official ethos was strong after his leadership of the development of a tank engine (the Meteor) from the Merlin aero-engine.

In March 1943, the Ministry of Supply wrote to Vickers relating that Ruston & Hornsby would be parent designer. Effectively Belper remained lead designer, while Ruston & Hornsby (which specialized in agricultural equipment) would be the co-developer and producer. Both should be blamed

1. VALENTINE I, 3RD TROOP, 'A' SQUADRON, 1ST ROYAL GLOUCESTERSHIRE HUSSARS, 20TH ARMOURED BRIGADE, 6TH ARMOURED DIVISION, IN ENGLAND, 1941

On 1 September 1940, Home Forces established 6th Armoured Division (AD) with 20th and 26th Armoured Brigades. By the start of November, 6AD had 123 Valentines – more than half of deliveries up to then. By February 1941, 6AD had 195 Valentines; by April it had 300; in September, during its final manoeuvres of the year, it had 340 tanks.

The assemblers had finished the tanks in khaki-green, over which the Army's workshops painted curvaceous patches in a darker shade. The unit has painted tactical signs in red, to denote the senior regiment in the brigade: the triangle denotes 'A' Squadron, within which is a number denoting the troop. On the offside nose of the tank is the transport weight; on the nearside nose and tail is painted the divisional sign; in the middle of the nose and tail, this unit was supposed to paint the number '51' in white – designating the senior armoured regiment – but this was not present on all vehicles.

2. VALENTINE III, 2ND TROOP, 'C' SQUADRON, 17TH/21ST LANCERS, IN TUNISIA, DECEMBER 1942

The Allied landings in Morocco and Algeria started on 8 November 1942. The most easterly landings were at Algiers. On 13 November, 6AD and 78th Infantry Division landed through Algiers, aiming for Tunis. 6AD had one Armoured Brigade (26th), with three armoured units: 16/5th Lancers, 17th/21st Lancers, and 2nd Lothians and Border Horse. Their left flank was screened by a battle group ('Blade Force'), whose main tank unit was 17th/21st Lancers, with a mix of Valentine IIIs and Crusader IIIs. Blade Force advanced 300 miles before being held up short of Tunis, when the battered units were returned to 6AD for the rest of the campaign.

In Britain, this tank was configured for 'Desert Service' with sand-coloured paint. For the greener conditions of Tunisia, patches of khaki have been painted. The unit has painted a number '2' on the left revolver port to denote the 2nd Troop, and a circle to denote 'C' Squadron, all in yellow to denote the middle regiment of the brigade in terms of seniority.

1

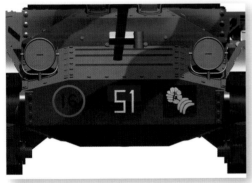

2

LEFT
The Valentine X had a coaxial machine-gun on the offside of the 6-pounder.

RIGHT
The Valentine XI's main armament was a 75mm gun, identifiable by its muzzle brake.

for the impractical driving and fighting arrangements, unnecessarily tall turret, and unnecessarily proud driver's compartment.

Belper planned delivery of three different pilots: Valiant I later in 1943, Valiant II around the end of 1943, and Heavy Valiant in 1944, with even thicker armour and the running gear common to the US T1/M6 heavy tank and the Heavy Cromwell. The Heavy Valiant was known, by various confused authorities, as Heavy Valiant, Valiant Mark III and Vanguard. Belper ignored the Tank Board's current requirement for a version with 17-pounder gun, and specified a 57mm 6-pounder gun, with allowance for a 75mm gun or a 95mm howitzer, each with coaxial machine-gun. For no good reason, Belper proposed an alternative armament of twin Oerlikon cannons with coaxial machine-gun, multiple machine-guns or machine-guns with a 20mm Oerlikon cannon.

Only one Valiant was produced, late in 1943 or early 1944 by Ruston & Hornsby. This survives with a 75mm gun, although possibly it had been assembled with a 57mm gun.

No report of the first trial survives, probably because it could not proceed safely. Vision through the periscopes was limited to 10 yards ahead. When changing down from fifth gear, the gear change lever came back so violently, with so little space between it and the right steering lever, that the driver might break his wrist in trying to operate it. (The Valiant steering levers were either side of the seat, instead of between the driver's knees.) The footbrake pedal was positioned such that the driver could depress it only with his heel, where it could become trapped between the pedal and the footplate. The driver was forced to sit in a crouched position that was liable to injure him by contact with the rear edge of the escape hatch.

There were other problems. The ground clearance was impractically low, as low as 8.75 inches below the final drive at the rear. Furthermore, the tail projected beyond the tracks, so the tank grounded on almost any rise.

The turret contained no stowage, no seats, and no turntable (just a wooden platform). Gunnery

The Valiant was replete with shot traps, the driver's hatches fouled the gun, and the driver's controls fouled each other.

would have been practically impossible, since the turret traverse control was fitted underneath the armament.

In April 1945, Ruston & Hornsby returned Valiant for trials of the suspension only, probably because Vickers had persuaded the Ministry of Supply that the suspension had been neglected, but a drive of 13 miles revealed the dangers, and the trial was abandoned. The suspension was too exposed and fragile for an assault tank anyway.

The School of Tank Technology retained the Valiant for the purpose of demonstrating to students how not to design a tank, before transferring it to the Tank Museum.

PRODUCTION

In May 1940, Vickers delivered a Valentine I for trials, which proved satisfactory, at which point it was recorded as a delivery (12 June). The Ministry of Supply counted ten deliveries by the end of June, 39 by the end of July.

Metropolitan-Cammell – a Vickers subsidiary – and BRCWC, both specializing in rolling stock, delivered one vehicle each for inspection in July

	Vickers	Metropolitan-Cammell	Birmingham Railway Carriage & Wagon Company (BRCWC)	Canadian Pacific Railway Company	Ruston & Hornsby	TOTAL new assemblies
Valentine I	175	66	67	0	0	308
Valentine II	350	494	667	0	0	1,511
Valentine III	0	0	536	0	0	536
Valentine IV	375	149	0	0	0	524
Valentine V	450	546	0	0	0	996
Valentine V DD	0	212	0	0	0	212
Valentine VI	0	0	0	30	0	30
Valentine VII	0	0	0	1,390	0	1,390
Valentine VIII	0	0	0	0	0	0
Valentine IX	965	122	0	0	0	1,087
Valentine IX DD	0	236	0	0	0	236
Valentine X	100	35	0	0	0	135
Valentine XI	100	20	0	0	0	120
Valentine XI DD	0	175	0	0	0	175
Valiant	0	0	0	0	1	1
Bishop	0	0	150	0	0	150
Archer	667	0	0	0	0	667
Bridgelayer	0	80	160	0	0	239
TOTAL	3,182	2,135	1,580	1,420	1	8,317

Orders and deliveries of Valentines and derivatives, by contractor and vehicle number

Assembler	Date of order	Orders	Deliveries	Period of delivery	WD numbers
Vickers	1 July 1939	275	175 Valentine I, 100 Valentine II	12 June 1940 to January 1942	T15946 to T16120 (Valentine I), T16121 to T16220 (Valentine II)
	31 May 1940	300	250 Valentine II, 50 Valentine V	29 February to 20 September 1941	T27121 to T27370 (Valentine II), T27371 to T27420 (Valentine V)
	13 December 1940	250 Valentine II	250 Valentine IV	By 22 September 1942	T47098 to T47347
	7 May 1941	755 Valentine III	125 Valentine IV, 400 Valentine V, 230 Valentine IX	1941 to 1942	T66466 to T66590 (Valentine IV), T66591 to T67220 (Valentine V and IX)
	7 October 1941	460 Valentine V	460 Valentine IX	By 4 January 1943	T122698 to T123157
	6 February 1942	475	275 Valentine IX, 100 Valentine X, 100 Valentine XI	By 23 September 1943	T123158 to T123632
	October (?) 1942	2 pilot Archers	2 pilot Archers	September to October 1943	S279594 to S279595
	November (?) 1943	800 Archers, reduced to 670, reduced to 665	665 Archers	May 1944 to September 1945	S279596 to S280260
	22 October 1942	500 Valiant/Vanguard, cancelled	0		
Metro-Cammell	29 June 1939	125 (67 Valentine I, 58 Valentine II)	44 Valentine I, 81 Valentine II	1 August 1940 to March 1941	T16221 to T16345
	2 November 1939	25 Valentine II	25 Valentine II	May to June 1941	T18071 to T18095
	28 December 1939	75 Valentine II	22 Valentine I, 53 Valentine II	14 October 1940 to March 1941	T20419 to T20440 (Valentine I); T20441 to T20493 (Valentine II)
	12 June 1940	300	214 Valentine II, 86 Valentine V	15 May to November 1941	T27421 to T27524, T27571 to T27674, T27679 to T27684 (Valentine II); T27525 to T27570, T27675 to T27678, T27685 to T27729 (Valentine V)
	6 March 1941	250 (101 Valentine II, 149 Valentine IV)	81 Valentine II, 20 Bridgelayer, 149 Valentine V	1941 to 1942	T32531 to T32595, T32685 to T32720 (Valentine II); T32471 to T32530, T32596 to T32684 (Valentine V)
	26 June 1941	645	40 Valentine II, 60 Bridgelayer, 460 Valentine V, 85 Valentine V DD	20 November 1941 to 11 March 1942	T67221 to T67260 (Valentine II), T67261 to T67320 (Bridgelayer), T67321 to T67865 (Valentine V)
	7 October 1941	455 (52 Valentine V, 75 Valentine V DD, 16 Valentine IX, 312 Valentine IX DD)	127 Valentine V DD, 92 Valentine IX, 236 Valentine IX DD	1942 to 1943	T82163 to T82617
	9 January 1942	460 Valentine V, reduced to 260 on 9 January 1943	30 Valentine IX, 35 Valentine X, 20 Valentine XI, 175 Valentine XI DD	1943 to 1944	T120690 to T120949
BRCWC	29 June 1939	70 Valentine I, 145 Valentine II	67 Valentine I, 133 Valentine II	3 August 1940 to 6 June 1941	T16356 to T16422 (Valentine I); T16423 to T16555 (Valentine II)
	2 November 1939	25	25 Valentine II	By May 1941	T17360 to T17384
	12 June 1940	300	299 Valentine II, 1 pilot Bishop	June to October 1941	T17385 to T17684 (Bishop was T17474)
	6 March 1941	250	210 Valentine II, 1 bullet-proof turret for pilot Bishop, 39 Bishop	1941 to 1942	T32721 to T32969 (Valentine II); random S-numbers including S32888 to S32969 (Bishop)
	26 June 1941	500 Valentine II	313 Valentine III, 77 Bridgelayer, 110 Bishop	By 26 May 1942	T59684 to T60183 (Valentine III and Bridgelayer); S59689 to S60029 (Bishop)
	7 October 1941	450, reduced to 305 on 9 January 1943	223 Valentine III, 82 Bridgelayer	By 11 February 1943	T121823 to T122127

1940. By the end of 1940, about 350 vehicles had been delivered, far more than expected. As of 2 August 1941, 1,156 Valentines had been accepted.

Vickers production peaked in December 1942 at 81 Valentines for the month, eased off most rapidly at the end of 1943, and ran out in May 1944, when production switched to the Archer, which ran out in September 1945.

In the end, 8,316 Valentine tanks and variants were produced (6,896 British and 1,420 Canadian), of which 7,260 were turreted tanks (5,840 British, 1,420 Canadian), of which 3,665 were exported to the Soviet Union (2,302 British, 1,388 Canadian), and two Canadian tanks were retained by

Britain. Thus, effectively, 3,540 Valentine turreted tanks were assembled on British account, 30 on Canadian account. Ruston & Hornsby assembled the only Valiant, for a total of 8,317 newly assembled vehicles developed from the Valentine platform.

USE

British use

In 1940 and 1941, the War Office allocated most Valentines to armoured divisions, pending deliveries of cruiser tanks. Their use as infantry tanks remained doubtful: the Matilda II was better protected; the Infantry Tank Mark IV (later known as 'Churchill') was under development with even thicker armour. Both accommodated three men in their turrets, unlike the Valentine, and were more mobile across country, although the Valentine was easier to transport and its automotive line was more mature.

Repeatedly, from November 1940 to June 1941, the Director of Armoured Fighting Vehicles (DAFV), Major-General Vyvyan Pope, recorded Valentines as stop-gaps, and denied their suitability as infantry tanks, mainly because of inferior protection, particularly due to the lack of skirts protecting the running gear.

At that time almost all Valentines were being used as stop-gap cruisers in three of the five armoured divisions at home. As of 1 May 1941, 772 Valentines were in service (307 Valentine Is; 465 Valentine IIs). As of 1 June 1941, 902 were in service, of which only four were overseas (for trials or demonstrations).

In June 1941, following a request from Middle East Command (ME or MEC) for more cruisers, Pope allowed for Valentines to be sent overseas as stop-gap cruisers, although the first 50 Valentine IIs enshipped as infantry tanks to replace the Matildas of 8th Battalion Royal Tank Regiment (RTR) that had been sunk in transit the previous month. They were not used in action until the next offensive in Libya codenamed as Operation *Crusader* (18 November 1941).

1st Army Tank Brigade's other two battalions (42nd and 44th RTR) were equipped with Matilda IIs, until replacement by Valentines during 1942. 7th RTR was converting from Matildas to Valentines when captured at Tobruk on 21 June 1942. A Special Service tank squadron (about 15 Valentines) was used during the invasion of Madagascar in May 1942.

By 21 June 1942, 660 Valentines had shipped to Egypt, although perhaps half had been knocked out or captured. For the offensive from Alamein (23 October 1942), 8th Army held 223 Valentines, of which 169 were employed by 23rd Armoured Brigade, whose four battalions supported infantry divisions as doctrinally prescribed. Another 20 Valentines

This Valentine II is configured for Desert Service with auxiliary fuel tank, sandguards over the tracks, and a container for five water cans on the rear; it has not yet been finished in sand-coloured paint. The tracks are of the third type, designed by the Department of Tank Design (DTD), with more links and single pins, for more reliability, but more weight. All later tanks, including all Canadian tanks, were delivered with this track. Most shoes were cast manganese steel, but some were stamped from slightly heavier 30-carbon steel, identifiable by slightly rounded ends.

This Valentine II in Egypt shows wear on the sides and gun due to the crew mounting and dismounting.

This Valentine XI is serving in north-west Europe as the command tank for a battalion of M10 Tank Destroyers.

were held by 8th Army as ready replacements, 31 were in repair, and three were training tanks. Another two Valentines had been evacuated on 21 October. As of 7 November, 23rd Armoured Brigade had lost 171 tanks: 19 tanks completely destroyed, 55 awaiting recovery, 29 in third-line workshops, and 68 already repaired and returned. This brigade was withdrawn from the frontline until 23 February 1943.

The 2-pounder, two-man turreted versions (Valentines II and IV) were still the most numerous versions through to the end of the North African campaign in May 1943. Late in 1942, Valentine IIIs and Vs (three-man turret) were issued to squadron and troop commanders. On 13 November 1942, 6th Armoured Division disembarked in the port of Algiers with Valentine IIIs and Crusader IIIs.

In December 1942, MEC's armoured warfare authority reported the Valentine as 'definitely obsolete' because of its thin armour and weak armament, even with the 6-pounder. Independently, MEC's technical authority reported:

> Valentine is an extremely dependable tank and mechanically superior to either Grant or Sherman petrol-engined tanks. As a fighting proposition it falls between two stools, being neither fast enough for a cruiser nor sufficiently well armoured for an assault tank. Of the two roles, the latter is the more suitable, as it is less likely to involve a conflict with enemy AFV, in which the tank has neither the striking power to make a stand nor the speed to get away.

These Valentine VIs are giving a flaming salute at Camp Borden in Canada.

Valentine IX tanks had arrived in January 1943, and first saw combat during the assault on the Mareth Line in Tunisia in March 1943, but 'also failed to find favour owing to their deficiency in fire power. From the point of view of reliability they were every bit as good as Sherman, and though less well protected in front, they had better side armour.'

By then, two tank brigades were ready in Tunisia with Churchill tanks, which carried the 6-pounder gun, a coaxial machine-gun, and a third crewman in the turret, and were better protected. These took the lead in subsequent assaults. By June 1943 the War Office had deleted Valentines from British tank units, although many remained in Soviet, Australian, New Zealand and Indian service, while British units in Europe retained Valentines as artillery observation vehicles (main armament removed), Bridgelayers, amphibious tanks, and tractors.

In New Zealand, a Valentine II is leading two Valentine IIIs or Vs, another Valentine II, and another Valentine III or V, ahead of a column of M3/M3A1 (Stuart) hybrids

Valentine XI tanks (with 75mm guns) were used by anti-tank battalion and battery commanders in the campaigns in north-west Europe and Italy from late 1944 onwards.

Canadian Valentines

The first Valentine VI was paraded for the press at Angus Works on 27 May 1941, although counted as a delivery in June, the only one for that month; this was followed by five more in July, ten in August and 14 in September, for a total of 30 (CT138916 to CT138945). 16 were held by the Armoured Corps School at Camp Borden, the other 14 apparently distributed to units. None was delivered in time for Canadian 1st Tank Brigade which enshipped for England in June 1941 without any tanks. There it was equipped with British tanks, until finally re-equipped with Churchills. In fact, 13 Canadian armoured units were in England by the end of 1941, most of which never trained with Valentines, apart from familiarization at Borden.

The 1,390 Valentine VIIs were allocated for export, starting in late November 1941: Britain retained two; 1,388 were enshipped to the Soviets, although only 1,208 arrived. In total, Canada produced 1,420 vehicles (73 in 1941, 943 in 1942 and 404 in 1943).

New Zealand use

In October 1941, 20 Valentine IIs arrived in New Zealand (NZ), ahead of Valentine IIIs, Valentine Vs and Matilda IV Close Support (CS) tanks. All were required for the 1st Army Tank Brigade, but this never filled, and was disbanded in October 1942, leaving 2nd Battalion with Valentine tanks and Stuart Hybrids (US M3 light tanks with M3A1 turrets), for service with the 3rd NZ Division in the Pacific Rim. (The NZ Division in North Africa was supported by British tank units.)

In 1943, 25 Valentine CS tanks were required for regional operations (19 to be issued to one squadron; six to be held by the Ordnance Field Park), although, due to lack of time before deployment, the requirement was reduced to 18.

Supplies of Valentines and derivatives to the USSR, by period and type

	October 1941 to June 1943			July 1943 to June 1944			TOTAL		
	Shipped	Lost at sea	Arrived	Shipped	Lost at sea	Arrived	Shipped	Lost at sea	Arrived
Valentine II	161	25	136	0	0	0	161	25	136
Valentine III	135	0	135	211	0	211	346	0	346
Valentine IV	520	71	449	0	0	0	520	71	449
Valentine V	234	113	121	106	0	106	340	113	227
Valentine VI–VII	1,213	170	1,043	175	10	165	1,388	180	1,208
Valentine IX	201	0	201	635	18	617	836	18	818
Valentine X	0	0	0	74	8	66	74	8	66
Bridgelayer	0	0	0	25	0	25	25	0	25
TOTAL	2,464	379	2,085	1,226	36	1,190	3,690	415	3,275

The first nine vehicles were converted from 1 to 19 August 1943, and issued to the Tank Squadron upon arrival in Wellington: two tanks were issued to the tank squadron HQ, one to each of the five troop leaders, and two to the Ordnance Field Park. The final nine were converted in September, and stayed in New Zealand. In early February 1944, the squadron landed in Guadalcanal with 25 Valentine IIIs, including nine CS. The squadron fought only one action, on 20 February 1944, when four CS tanks were engaged.

Soviet use

The General Staff had already declared the Valentine obsolete when the British government expanded production as aid to the Soviet Union after the Axis invasion of 22 June 1941. On 24 August 1941, the Ministry of Supply asked (as a courtesy) for the War Office's agreement to order another 1,325

B

1. VALENTINE IX OF 50TH ROYAL TANK REGIMENT, IN TUNISIA, MARCH 1943

Valentine IX tanks arrived in North Africa in January 1943, but saw no operational use until the assault on the Mareth Line in Tunisia. On 16 March, infantry captured the approaches to the Wadi Zigzaou. At 2315 hours on 20 March, 9th Battalion, Durham Light Infantry (DLI), of 50th Division, advanced over the wadi to the strongpoint of Ksiba Ouest, while 8th DLI advanced to Ouerzi – one mile to the left (west). In between, 50th RTR, with Valentines – a few of which were Valentine IXs, was supposed to advance into the rear of both positions, after which 6th DLI was supposed to consolidate. The tanks moved forward in the early hours of 21 March. Under increasing artillery fire, the engineers blew gaps in the wadi, and constructed a causeway with fascines and earth, but only three tanks gained traction up the muddy bank before the causeway collapsed under the fourth tank. The other tanks withdrew at first light, hoping for another attempt on the following night. At 2330 hours, 5th East Yorkshires advanced to the right of Ksiba Ouest, while 9th DLI expanded its lodgement, and 6th DLI advanced to strongpoints behind Ouerzi, but 50th RTR again failed to get across. At 0145 hours 22 March, 15th Panzer Division drove back the Valentines, while the infantry took cover in the wadi with high casualties. Before dawn on 23 March, 50th Division completed its withdrawal.

2. VALENTINE XI OF 2ND ANTI-TANK REGIMENT ROYAL CANADIAN ARTILLERY, 2ND CANADIAN INFANTRY DIVISION, IN GERMANY, FEBRUARY 1945

2nd Canadian Infantry Division was mobilized at the start of the war, and deployed to Britain from August to December 1940. After its bloody baptism at Dieppe on 19 August 1942 (where the only Allied tanks were Churchills), it did not see combat again until after landing in Normandy in July 1944. Thereafter, it was one of the leading 'assault' divisions in almost every operation, so in October its anti-tank regiment was prioritized for Archers, which were accompanied by Valentine XI tanks for use by each of the four battery commanders. These vehicles were incorporated during the division's long period of deserved rest from November 1944 to January 1945. This Valentine XI was used on the first day of Operation *Veritable* (the offensive into the Rhineland) on 8 February 1945, when the division was tasked with assaults on Wyler and Den Heuvel.

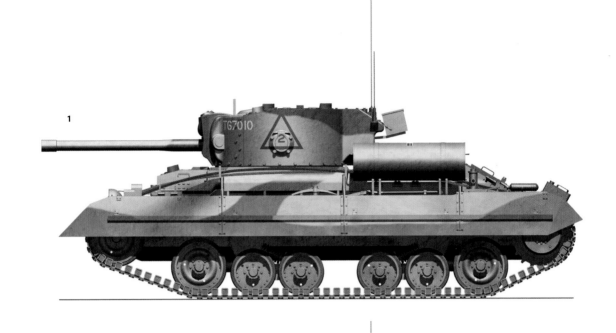

1

2

Valentines, for total production of 5,600 Valentines through July 1943.

On 28 October 1941, the first 20 Valentines arrived at the tank training school in Kazan, while another 120 were unloading at Arkhangel'sk. As of 20 November, the Soviets had issued 97 Valentines to six tank battalions (131st had 21 Valentines, 132nd had 19, 136th had 9, 138th had 6, and 137th and 139th, both of 146th Tank Brigade, had 21 Valentines each). By the end of 1941, the Soviets had unloaded 259 Valentines and issued 216.

The Soviets preferred their own tanks, followed by the Matilda II, so relegated the Valentine to defensive operations during summer 1942 against second-rate enemies.

By then, Canadian Valentines were arriving quicker. In the second half of 1942, Canada shipped 298 Valentine VIIs directly to Russia, followed by 460 in the first half of 1943, and 155 in the second half.

The Soviets attempted to install a 76.2mm gun, and manufactured stronger track pins and spurs to help traction in winter conditions, to which the Canadians responded with a track fitted with small 'ice spikes', and other minor changes, which were standardized on the Valentine VIIa.

British Valentine IXs and Xs arrived in 1943, and remained in Soviet use through to the end of the war, but always in second-rate units. In total, 3,690 Valentine platforms were sent, equivalent to 71 per cent of all British and Canadian platforms sent.

The first batch of Valentine VIs for the Soviet Union was entrained at Angus Works in Montreal on 18 November 1941, with dashed lines containing loading information that the Soviets rarely obscured.

Amphibious Valentines
Valentine DD

Early in 1942, Nicolas Straussler converted a Valentine II to the amphibious configuration later known as Duplex Drive (DD); another was converted with an adapted flotation screen. Both were destroyed during trials. Metropolitan-Cammell subsequently converted another two Valentine IIs, of which the last became the final design. None of these conversions was counted in DD production.

These Valentine V DDs are training near Gosport in January 1944. The turret would be traversed to the rear when raising the screens.

The trackguards were replaced by a platform extending around the hull, fabricated from mild steel plates, welded together into sections that were bolted to the tank's hull. The platform was braced by angle iron struts atop the platform. Another two struts on the underside of the platform at the rear protected the propeller.

On a flange on the outer edge of this platform was erected the screen, secured by steel beading bolted to the flange by countersunk bolts, the joint being made watertight by strips of sponge rubber.

The screen was constructed from rubberized flax canvas and supported by 33 pneumatic tubes that made up 'air pillars'; 16 long pillars extended from the air base to the top frame of the canvas, 17 short pillars to the lower frame.

The support was completed by two tubular frames running around the inside of the screen, and four mechanical struts (two each side of the vehicle).

The total displacement was about 600 cubic feet, with the entire hull below the waterline.

The propeller was a three-bladed, right-handed prop, 24.5 inches in diameter, with a pitch of 16 inches, driven by a power take-off from the rear of the transmission, giving a vehicle speed afloat of up to 4.5mph.

The driver could steer via hydraulic linkages, by swivelling the propeller within a universal joint contained within a spherical housing, to which was attached a stub axle pivoted on fulcrum pins at top and bottom of the housing. The joint between housing and stub axle was closed by a spring-tensioned oil seal.

By similar hydraulic linkages, the driver could tilt the propeller up to prevent damage when the vehicle was out of the water. A mechanical lock held the propeller in the raised position.

During assembly, the hull was waterproofed with Bostik compounds up to the level of the platform. Joints between sections of the platform and between the platform and the hull were made watertight with sponge rubber strips and Bostik adhesive. However, Bostik deteriorated with age, running, and contact with fuels or hydraulic fluid, so older vehicles were reserved for training on land.

This Valentine V is driving off a landing craft, with the propeller raised until the tail clears the ramp.

Use

In summer 1942, the General Staff ordered 450 Valentine DDs. In the end, Metropolitan-Cammell assembled 623 Valentine DDs (212 Valentine V DDs, 236 Valentine IX DDs and 175 Valentine XI DDs). The added equipment was the same in all cases.

Most were retained in England for training. By then the Sherman DD was clearly more seaworthy, roomier and better armed, but due to the late acquisition of Sherman DDs, some British units trained with Valentine DDs at Frinton-on-Sea as late as May 1944, even though only Sherman DDs would land in Normandy in June 1944. British units generally trained with Valentine DDs in inland waters before taking Sherman DDs to sea,

although Valentine DDs were used during the largest Allied amphibious exercise ('Exercise *Smash 1*' at Studland Bay, Dorset, on 4 April 1944), when six Valentine DDs sank (all operated by 4th/7th Royal Dragoon Guards), causing six fatalities.

In late 1943, 105 Valentine IX DDs were sent to Italy, where 75 of them were considered operational, the other 30 being reserved for training.

As late as mid-1945, Valentine DDs were the only DDs in India and Burma, but none was used in an opposed landing. British forces there were still converting to Sherman DDs when Japan surrendered.

Self-propelled guns
Bishop

This newly delivered Bishop gives a true impression of the high profile of the superstructure. The gunner's ports are closed; the driver's visor is open.

In June 1941, the DAFV (Pope) required 'assault artillery', meaning self-propelled direct-fire weapons, inspired by the 'startling successes gained by the German assault artillery'. The requirements for direct and indirect fire could be filled by one weapon – the 25-pounder gun/howitzer. In June 1941, the Ministry of Supply asked BRCWC to develop a self-propelled 25-pounder on a Valentine platform. In August, this was ready for firing trials at Shoeburyness, Essex.

On 9 September 1941, the Tank Board agreed to place a requirement for 100 vehicles 'as soon as the design had been approved'. The Minister of Supply stated that the vehicles could be produced by December 1941 if the order were given at once. On 4 November, an order for 100 vehicles was placed, but on 12 December, the Chief of the Imperial General Staff (Alan Brooke) chaired a meeting on all self-propelled artillery projects (25-pounder

C

VALENTINE IIS OF 23RD ARMOURED BRIGADE ATTACK RUWEISAT RIDGE, EGYPT, 22 JULY 1942

In May 1942, 8th Armoured Division enshipped from Britain, with Valentine tanks in lieu of cruiser tanks. While 24th Armoured Brigade was delayed by its ship's engine trouble, 23rd Armoured Brigade disembarked on 6 July with orders to prepare as an army tank brigade. 50th RTR soon was diverted for use as an independent battalion, leaving the brigade with two battalions (40th and 46th RTR), each with 49 Valentines and three Matilda II Close Support tanks. The brigade's two headquarters tanks added in for a total of 106 tanks. On 22 July, the brigade was committed to an attack on Point 59 and the escarpment of El Mreir, despite failure of an attempt the previous night to seize Point 63 to the north. All these points lay on the slight rise known as Ruweisat Ridge. At 0800 hours, the Brigade attacked with 46th RTR on the left and 40th on the right. They advanced in columns, ready to enter cleared gaps (just 30 yards wide) in the minefield. Leading tanks strayed on to mines before the gaps were found, and came under anti-tank fire. Those tanks that crossed the minefield then advanced on Point 59. Unknowingly, 40th RTR overran II Battalion of 104th Panzergrenadier Regiment, just short of Afrikakorps HQ, but other Germans continued to fight, most notably the crew of one 76.2mm gun that knocked out nine Valentines. A counter-attack by 21st Panzer Division restored the German positions. By 1030 hours, 23rd Armoured Brigade was left with only 15 running tanks, of which only 12 could operate their 2-pounder guns. 7th Rifle Brigade, which had deployed 1,500 yards short of the objective, decided to withdraw. Only seven Valentines completed the withdrawal, around 1230 hours.

In Tunisia in 1943, a troop of muddy Bishops has taken position on a slope, which will help to increase range.

on Valentine; 6-inch howitzer on Churchill; 3-inch 20-hundredweight in Churchill 'Special Type'). After reading the Ministry's view that the Valentine was too small and light, Brooke directed that the Valentine 25-pounder order should be reduced to 60, 'if this could be done economically and without upsetting production. The equipments should be tried out and used in the Middle East and kindred theatres and a report should be rendered on their suitability for desert action.'

Over winter 1941–1942, Allied forces started to use more 25-pounders in direct fire support, but this increased the guns' exposure and prevented their ready concentration for indirect fire. Thus, the requirement for self-propelled 25-pounders was more urgent by spring 1942. In July 1942, the order was extended to a cumulative total of 150.

Production started in March 1942, using the platform of the Valentine III. Deliveries seem to have been completed by May 1942. Bishops were first used in Egypt in October 1942. Already, Allied units there were using US M7

This Bishop in 'Desert Service' configuration is undergoing trials in Egypt. This view shows the limited elevation of the 25-pounder.

The Bishop's fighting compartment does not look as spacious inside as outside. Ammunition occupied most of the side walls, in two rows. The recoil normally varied between 16 and 19 inches, although the recoil strip was graduated from 10 to 24 inches. Cartridge cases were expended through a chute into the lowest part of the compartment, behind the driver. The gunner sat on a fixed leather-covered seat to the left. Behind him, the loader could sit in a tip-up, leather-covered seat –this pivoted vertically and was normally clamped into a bracket on the left wall. The commander could sit on a similar seat to the right. The gun was fired with the rear doors open, for ventilation, and to allow for resupply from the trailer over the engine deck.

SP 105mm howitzers ('Priests'), which offered superior throw-weight, stowage and reliability. On 20 June 1943, 8th Army's technical authority reported that the Bishop 'was found to be quite unsuitable and was scrapped. The chief disadvantages were the limits of both range and traverse.' However, other units continued to use Bishops in Italy until they were scrapped in 1944, leaving no surviving vehicles anywhere.

Archer

On 25 June 1942, the General Staff agreed that the Ministry of Supply should explore self-propelled 6-pounder, 17-pounder or 3-inch 20-hundredweight anti-tank guns, or 25-pounder field guns/howitzers, using the platforms of the Matilda II, Valentine, Cruiser VI (Crusader) or Cruiser VII tanks. On 14 August, the AFV Division of the Ministry of Supply submitted its proposals to the War Office and on 16 September the War Office required 400 self-propelled anti-tank guns, 1,000–1,500 self-propelled field guns and 2,000 infantry guns. On 6 October, the two ministries agreed to develop a self-

This display illustrates the Archer's advantages and disadvantages compared to the M10 Tank Destroyer at left, and the 'Alecto'. The Archer has a lower silhouette than the M10, and mounted the most powerful gun. Although the M10 could be rearmed with the same gun (to produce the 'Achilles'), its fighting compartment was smaller. The M10 had a fully traversing turret, although the Archer's 45 degrees of traverse was plenty in most defensive positions. The Archer offered the best mobility off road. None of these vehicles was assembled with a complete roof, although separate kits were produced later to rectify the M10 and Archer.

This Archer is protecting the flank of a road near Nutterden, on 9 February 1945 – the second day of the offensive into the Rhineland. The crewmen have thrown the cover over the mounting, on top of which they have rested the Bren. They have gathered stowage towards the front to clear the arc of fire.

propelled 17-pounder gun (eventually Archer) and a 25-pounder (eventually Bishop) on the Valentine platform, and a self-propelled 95mm gun/howitzer (eventually the useless 'Alecto') on the Light Tank Mark VIII platform.

The Archer was piloted in September 1943, before a second pilot, which was accepted for production, although this was delayed by production of tanks for Soviet receipt until May 1944 (26 Archers). Production peaked in September (63), and reached 349 for the year. Another 178 were produced in the first third of 1945. Upon the surrender of Japan in August, the order for 800 vehicles was reduced, allowing for the 665th vehicle to be completed in September.

Archers were used by anti-tank battalions within prioritized infantry divisions in Italy and north-west Europe from October 1944. Archers replaced US M10 Tank Destroyers in the assault infantry divisions of north-west Europe towards the end of 1944, and replaced towed guns in the other frontline infantry divisions early in 1945.

Users liked its cross-country performance and reliability, particularly in mud and uphill climbs. The Archer's rear-heaviness actually improved its cross-country mobility compared to the tank; however, the Archer was not as fast or reliable as the M10 on hard roads.

The gun was mounted with limited traverse, facing backwards, which meant that the Archer backed into a firing position, although users liked

D

1. VALENTINE VI AT THE CANADIAN ARMOUR SCHOOL AT BORDEN CAMP, CANADA, IN 1942

The first Valentine VI was paraded for the press on 27 May 1941. The second vehicle was delivered in July, and probably sent straight to the Royal Canadian Armoured Corps School at Camp Borden in Ontario to familiarize personnel with the type.

2. VALENTINE VI, SOVIET 139TH TANK BATTALION, 146TH TANK BRIGADE, IN RUSSIA, 1942

British Valentine IIs first reached the Soviet Union in October 1941. 139th Tank Battalion was the last of the six battalions to be issued with Valentine IIs that year. In 1942, it received Valentine VIs from Canada. Most of these tanks went into action as received. With time and experience, this unit painted tactical numbers on the sides. After the first snowfall, the tanks were whitewashed.

1

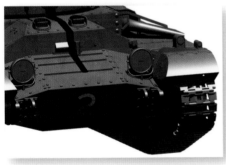

2

	Specification, 14 April 1939	Valentine I	Valentine II	Valentine III	Valentine IV	Valentine V	Valentine VI and VII	Valentine IX	Valentine X	Valentine XI
Weight, laden (inc. crew)*	16.00 long tons (17.92 short; 16.26 metric)	17.05 long tons (19.10 short; 17.32 metric)						17.20 long tons (19.26 short; 17.48 metric)		
Length**	17ft 9in (5.41m)	17ft 9.5in (5.42m) to tracks; 18ft 9.7in (5.73m) to sandguards						19ft 5in (5.92m) to 6-pdr Mark III muzzle at front and sandguard at rear; 20ft 9in (6.32m) to 6-pdr Mark V muzzle		20ft 10.625in (6.37m) to muzzle at front and sandguard at rear
Width †	8ft 5in (2.57m)	8ft 5in (2.57m) to tracks; 8ft 7.5in (2.63m) to track guards; 9ft 1in (2.77m) to sandguards								
Height ††	7ft 2in (2.18m)	6ft 7.6in (2.02m) to top of turret; 6ft 10.5in (2.10m) to periscope cover; 7ft 5.5in (2.27m) to top of sighting vane	7ft 3.5 (2.22m) to periscope cover	As Valentine I	7ft 3.5 (2.22m) to periscope cover	As Valentine I		6ft 11.5in (2.12m) to periscope cover; 7ft 1in (2.16m) to sighting vane		
Engine type	AEC A189	AEC A189 9.64 liter, 6-cylinder, spark ignition	AEC A190 (diesel version of A189)		GMC 6-71S (Model 6004 "S" type) 6.96 liter, 6-cylinder, diesel			GMC 6-71S (Model 6004 "S" type) or 6-71A (Model 6004 "A" type)	GMC 6-71A (Model 6004 "A" type)	
Torque (lb-in.)	-	4,960 at 1,000 rpm; 4,920 at 1,200 rpm	4,980 at 1,250 rpm		5,460 at 900 rpm			5,460 at 900 rpm ("S" Type); 6,300 at 1,000 rpm ("A" type)	6,300 at 1,000 rpm	
Engine power (brake horse power)	150 at 2,000 rpm	135 at 1,900 rpm (governed speed)	131 at 1,800 rpm		130 at 1,900 rpm			130 at 1,900 rpm ("S" Type); 165 at 1,900 rpm ("A" type)	165 at 1,900 rpm	
Power/weight ratio (bhp per long ton)	9.4	7.9	7.7		7.6			7.56 ("S" Type); 9.6 ("A" type)	9.6	
Main gearbox, type	-	Meadows Number 22 (clash), 5 forward, 1 reverse			Spicer (syncromesh and clash), 5 forward, 1 reverse					
Steering	-	Clutch and brake, operated mechanically by steering levers; multi-disc clutch and epicyclic double reduction gears in final drive, minimum turning circle 13ft (3.96m)								
Brakes	-	Internal expanding shoes (4), by Girling, with nickel-chrome steel drums, with bonded asbestos linings by Ferodo								
Suspension	Coil spring and hydraulic shock absorber (by Newton) acting on 3 wheels at a time ("slow motion" system)									
Tracks	Six road wheels each side; track width14in (0.36m)									
Ground pressure (lb/ sq. in)	-	10.5	11.15					11.3 (11.5 for DD)		

* DD Valentines weighed 17.50 long tons (19.60 short; 17.78 metric)
** with DD screens, Valentines measured 20ft 3in (6.17m)
† DD, Valentines measured 9ft 5in (2.87 m) to DD skirts
†† with DD screens raised, Valentines measured 9ft 7in (2.92m) at front, 9ft 3in (2.82m) at rear, 7ft 10in (2.39m) at sides

being able to drive forward out of trouble. They liked the low silhouette and the well-arranged fighting compartment, although they disliked the thin armour, the incomplete overhead protection, and the exhaust smoke that gave them away when changing positions.

CAPABILITIES

Driving
Access
The driver sat centrally, with two doors either side, opening up to the sides. Each door was sprung by torsion bars to assist opening and closing. The door

	Valentine Bridgelayer	Valentine Scorpion (UK Scorpion Mark III)	Valentine Carrier 25-pounder (later: "Bishop")	Archer as delivered in 1944	Valiant "Assault tank" as proposed by Vickers in 1942	Valiant as piloted by Rolls-Royce and Ruston & Hornsby in 1943	Heavy Valiant as designed by Rolls-Royce and Ruston & Hornsby in March 1944
Weight, laden (inc. crew)*	19.25 long tons (21.56 short; 19.56 metric)	unknown	17.50 long tons (19.60 short; 17.78 metric)	16.50 long tons (18.48 short; 16.76 metric)	23.00 long tons (25.76 short; 23.37 metric)	26.90 long tons (30.13 short; 27.33 metric)	42.27 long tons (47.34 short; 42.95 metric)
Length	23ft 7in (7.19m)	27ft 0in (8.23m)	As Valentine III	18ft 8in (5.69m) to trackguards; 21ft 11.25in (6.69m) with gun	17ft 7in (5.36m) without gun; 18ft 4in (5.59m) with gun	16ft 10in (5.13m) without gun; 17ft 4.5in (5.30m) with gun	20ft 10in (6.35m) with 57mm gun forward; 19ft 4in (5.89m) with gun aft
Width	9ft 8.25in (2.95m)	11ft 10in (3.61m)	As Valentine III	8ft 5.5in (2.58m) to tracks; 9ft 0.5in (2.76m) to trackguards	9ft 3in (2.81m)	9ft 5.5in (2.88m) to trackguards	10ft 7.75in (3.24m) to detachable final drive cover plates; 10ft 1.75in (3.09m) to side skirts
Height	11ft 3in (3.43m)	8ft 3in (2.54m)	10ft (3m)	7ft 3in (2.21m) to top of mounting, 7ft 4.5in (2.25m) to top of sloped roof	7ft 0in (2.13m) to periscope cover	7ft 5.5in (2.27m) to turret roof plate; 8ft 1in (2.46m) to aerial base	8ft 2.4in (2.50m) to periscope cover
Engine type	AEC A190 9.64 litre diesel			GMC 6-71M 6.96 litre diesel	GMC 6-71M (Valiant 1) or Rolls-Royce Meteorite V8 (Valiant II)	GMC 6-71M 6.96 litre diesel	Rolls-Royce Meteorite V8
Torque (lb-in.)	4,980 at 1,250 rpm			6,624 at 1400 rpm	11,160 (Meteorite) or 6,624 at 1400 rpm (GMC)	6,624 at 1400 rpm	6,458 at 1,500 rpm
Engine power (brake horse power)	131 at 1,800 rpm			192 at 1,900 rpm	400 (Meteorite) or 210 at 2200 rpm(GMC)	210 at 2,200 rpm	330 at 2,200 rpm
Power/weight ratio (bhp per long ton)	6.7	unknown	7.5	11.6	17.4 (valiant I) or 19.6 (Valiant II)	7.8	
Main gearbox, type	Meadows Number 22 (clash), 5 forward, 1 reverse			Spicer (syncromesh and clash), 5 forward, 1 reverse			Merritt-Brown Z5, 5 forward, 1 reverse
Steering	Clutch and brake, operated mechanically by steering levers; multi-disc clutch and epicyclic double reduction gears in final drive						Controlled differential
Turning circle	13ft (3.96m) minimum				unknown		
Brakes	Internal expanding shoes (4), by Girling, with nickel-chrome steel drums, with bonded asbestos linings by Ferodo				Internal expanding (Vickers had specified external contracting in the first proposal of June 1942)		
Suspension	Coil spring and hydraulic shock absorber (by Newton) acting on 3 wheels at a time ("slow motion" system)				Independent concentric coils acting on each wheel		HVSS acting on 2 wheels at a time
Roadwheels	Six each side						
Track width	14in (0.36m)				20in (0.51m)		25.5in (0.65m)
Ground pressure (lb/ sq. in)	12.6	unknown	11.5	10.3	10.5	unknown	13.6

could be locked in the closed position by a bolt, or retained in the open position by another bolt. The door was supposed to be locked, otherwise the motion of a door swinging to and fro would wear out the torsion bars. The doors could not be opened from the outside.

To access the emergency hatch below, the driver would need to vacate his seat to the offside, fold the back rest forward on top of the seat, grasp the whole seat and swing it up to the vertical position, and release the hatch's two locking levers. At this point, the door was supposed to fall away, although it could remain stuck if buckled by blast or heat. To move between the driver's compartment and the fighting compartment the driver would need to lay the seat's backrest flat.

Vision

The driver had two periscopes – one looking forward right, one looking forward left – and a rectangular aperture in the front vertical plate, closed by a visor. The right-hand periscope could be rotated freely, but was supposed

Specification, 14 April 1939		Valentine I	Valentine II	Valentine III	Valentine IV	Valentine V	Valentine VI and VII	Valentine IX	Valentine X	Valentine XI
Speed, max	15mph (24.1km/h)									
Fording	-	3ft (0.91m)								
Vertical step	-	3ft (0.91m)								
Clearance under hull	16.5in (0.42m)	16.5in (0.42m) centre, 8in (0.20m) under suspension bracket								
Horizontal gap	7ft 6in (2.29m)	7ft 9in (2.36m)								
Gradient or slope (degrees)	-	32								
Fuel tanks capacity (imperial gallons)*	As tested: 26+26	31+31 (2.5 gals unusable)		31 + 5 (2.5 gals unusable	40 (2.5 gals unusable)			46	40	
Operational range per gallon, road	-	1.16 miles (1.87km)		3.14 miles (5.05km)	2.5 miles (4.02km)					
Operational range per gallon, across country	-	0.82 miles (1.32km)		1.9 miles (3.06km)	1.5 miles (2.41km)					
Operational range on road	70 miles (112.7km)	102 miles (164.1km)		199 miles (320.3km)	158 miles (254.3km)					
Operational range across country	(terrain not specified)	72 miles (115.9km)		121 miles (194.7km)	95 miles (152.9km)					

* auxiliary tank gave 32.5 gallons, of which 30 were useable

	Valentine Bridgelayer	Valentine Scorpion (UK Scorpion Mark III)	Valentine Carrier 25-pounder (later: "Bishop")	Archer as delivered in 1944	Valiant "Assault tank" as proposed by Vickers in 1942	Valiant as piloted by Rolls-Royce and Ruston & Hornsby in 1943	Heavy Valiant as designed by Rolls-Royce and Ruston & Hornsby in March 1944
Speed, maximum	10mph (16.1km/h)	15mph (24.1km/h)		21mph (33.8km/h)	16mph (25.7km/h) for Valiant I; 20mph (32.2km/h) for Valiant II	unknown	13mph (20.9km/h)
Fording	3ft (0.91m)						
Vertical step	3ft (0.91m)			2ft 9in (0.84m)	3ft (0.91m)	Unknown	2ft 6in (0.76m)
Clearance under hull	16.5in (0.42m) centre, 8in (0.20m) under suspension bracket				Unknown	17.65in (0.45m) at centre front to 8.75in (0.22m) at rear suspension bracket	Unknown
Horizontal gap	7ft 9in (2.36m)	Unknown	7ft 9in (2.36m)		8ft 0in (2.44m)	Unknown	7ft 6in (2.29m)
Gradient or slope (degrees)	32	Unknown	32		30	Unknown	33
Fuel tanks capacity (imperial gallons)	36 + 30	31 + 5 (2.5 gallons unusable)		50	Unknown		63
Operational range per gallon, road	Unknown			2.9 miles (4.67km)	Unknown		
Operational range per gallon, across country	Unknown	1.41 miles (1.83km)		1.5 miles (2.41km)	Unknown		
Operational range on road	150 miles (241.4km)	Unknown		140 miles (225.3km)	100 miles (160.9km) (terrain not specified)		60 miles (96.6km) (terrain not specified)
Operational range across country (miles)	Unknown	47 miles (76km)		75 miles (120.7km)			

to be aimed at the rear-view mirror on the right trackguard. As a precaution, the periscopes could be remounted back to front to present the armoured backside of the mounting to the enemy.

In all the Valentines, the visor could be swung out to the side, controlled from the inside by a lever. If open, the driver was protected by a 'look-out block'. The look-out block was considered an emergency option if the periscopes were damaged and the driver was unable to repair them. This consisted of a bullet-proof shield, with four vision slits, in front of a Triplex block. In case of damage, the whole look-out block could be lowered by

	Specification, 14 April 1939	Valentine I	Valentine II	Valentine III	Valentine IV	Valentine V	Valentine VI and VII	Valentine IX	Valentine X	Valentine XI
main armament	Royal Ordnance 40mm 2-pdr Mark IX or Mark X (76mm howitzer in Mark III CS)							Royal Ordnance 57mm 6-pdr gun Mark III or Mark V		75mm gun Mark V
rounds for main armament	50	53	60	62x 40mm or 35x 76mm	62			53	44	46
coaxial MG	7.92mm calibre Besa MG Number 1 Mark 1 or Mark 2 with 3,150 rounds (14 boxes)							None	7.92mm Besa MG Number 1 Mark 2 with 1,575 rounds (7 boxes; 11 boxes on later vehicles)	7.92mm Besa MG Number 1 Mark 2 with 2,700 rounds (12 boxes)
anti-aircraft armament	0.303in (7.7mm) calibre Bren LMG Mark I or II, with 6x 100-round drums									
personal weapons	0.45in (11.43mm) Thompson SMG stowed with 8x 20-round magazines (or 9mm Sten with 8x 30 round magazines from Valentine X onwards); revolvers on some crewmen									
smoke, obfuscatory	either one internal or two external smokes dischargers	2-inch smoke projector with 18 bombs; 9 hand grenades (some mix of smoke or fragmentation)						two 4-inch smoke dischargers, Number 2, Mark I, and two smoke generators, Number 8 Mark II or Mark III, with 6 rounds; 6 (Mark X) or 9 (Mark XI) hand grenades (some mix of smoke or fragmentation)		
turret mounting	-	2-pdr Number 5 Mark I or II		2-pdr Number 7 Mark I	2-pdr Number 5 Mark I or II	2-pdr Number 7 Mark I	2-pdr Number 5 Mark I or II	6-pdr/75mm Number 1 Mark 1	6-pdr/75mm Number 4 Mark 1	6-pdr/75mm Number 1 Mark 1 or Number 2
gunner's sight	-	Number 30 Mark I, Number 30 Mark IA, Number 33 Mark I, or Number 33IS telescopic						Number 39, Mark I or Mark II, telescopic		Number 50, Mark I or Mark II telescopic
main armament traverse	360 degrees, electric and manual geared control system by Lucas									
main armament elevation/depression	elevation 20 degrees, depression 15 degrees (5 degrees at rear); controlled freely by shoulder piece							elevation 17 degrees, depression 8 degrees, or 5 degrees at rear; by geared handwheel (MG could be moved freely via the pistol grip after releasing a locking catch)		
crew	3			4	3	4	3			

	Valentine Bridgelayer	Valentine Scorpion (UK Scorpion Mark III)	Valentine Carrier 25-pounder (later: "Bishop")	Archer as delivered in 1944	Valiant "Assault tank" as proposed by Vickers in 1942	Valiant as piloted by Rolls-Royce and Ruston & Hornsby in 1943	Heavy Valiant as designed by Rolls-Royce and Ruston & Hornsby in March 1944
main armament	None		87.6mm 25-pdr gun/howitzer Mark II	76mm 17-pdr gun Mark II	57mm 6-pdr gun	75mm gun Mark V	57mm 6-pdr gun, 75mm gun, or 95mm howitzer
rounds for main armament	None		32 inside	39	55	Unknown	50
coaxial MG	None	None	None	None	7.92mm Besa MG with 1,800 rounds		
anti-aircraft armament	0.303in (7.7mm) calibre Bren LMG Mark I or II, with 6x 100-round drums		Unknown	0.303in (7.7mm) calibre Bren LMG with 24x 30-round magazines	Unknown		
personal weapons	Thompson or Sten SMG stowed with 10 magazines		Thompson SMG with 16 magazine	2 Sten SMGs with no magazines except those on crew	Unknown		
smoke, obfuscatory	9 hand grenades (some mix of smoke or fragmentation)		Unknown	One 2-inch mortar Mark VIII, and four smoke generators, Number 8, with 18 rounds (nominally illumination rounds, potentially smoke); no grenades	2-inch mortar with 18 bombs		
turret mounting	None		25-pdr Valentine, Mark I	17-pdr SP Number 1 Mark 1	Unknown		
gunner's sight	None		Telescopic, dial, and clinometer	Number 51 Mark I, telescopic; Number 10 dial sight; clinometer sight Mark IV	Unknown		
main armament traverse	None		4 degrees right and left	45 degrees (22.5 each side of longitudinal centre line), by handwheel, with electrical power assistance	360 degrees, electric and manual geared control system by Lucas		
main armament elevation/depression	None		Elevation 15 degrees, depression 5 degrees	Elevation 15 degrees, depression 7.5 degrees; by handwheel	Unknown		Elevation 20 degrees, depression 12 degrees
crew	2	3	4		3		

	Specification, 14 April 1939	Valentine I	Valentine II	Valentine III	Valentine IV	Valentine V	Valentine VI and VII	Valentine IX	Valentine X	Valentine XI
Hull nose	60mm basis (60mm rolled or 65mm cast)	60mm; 20mm to floor								
Hull glacis		30mm								
Driver plate		60mm								
Hull sides		60mm vertical; 30mm sloping sides of engine compartment		50mm vertical; 30mm sloping sides of engine compartment				43mm vertical; 30mm sloping sides of engine compartment		
Hull rear		17mm towards roof; 60mm vertical; 17mm sloping towards floor								
Hull floor		20mm under driver's compartment; 7mm rearwards								
Hull roof		20mm above driver; 30mm sloping sides of engine compartment; 17mm louvres and covers; 10mm roof elsewhere								
Turret or superstructure front and mantlet		65mm						65mm turret front and bottom mantlet; 41mm upper mantlet; 14mm MG cover plate		
Turret sides		60mm								
Turret rear		65mm						65mm vertical, 32mm sloped upper		
Turret roof		20mm forwards, 10mm centre, 15mm rearwards								20mm, exce 10mm rearwards

	Valentine Bridgelayer	Valentine Scorpion (UK Scorpion Mark III)	Valentine Carrier 25-pounder (later: "Bishop")	Archer as delivered in 1944	Valiant "Assault tank" as proposed by Vickers in 1942	Valiant as piloted by Rolls-Royce and Ruston & Hornsby in 1943	Heavy Valiant as designed by Rolls-Royce and Ruston & Hornsby in March 1944
Hull nose	60mm; 20mm to floor			20mm; 10mm sloping to floor	114mm (4.5in) basis		216mm (8.5in)
Hull glacis	30mm			20mm	114mm (4.5in) basis		114mm (4.5in)
Driver plate	60mm			20mm	114mm (4.5in) basis		229mm (9in)
Hull sides	60mm vertical; 30mm sloping sides of engine compartment		50mm vertical; 30mm sloping sides of engine compartment	20mm	102mm (4in) basis		140mm (5.5in) forward, 127mm (5in) around engine compartment (including 1in skirt)
Hull rear	17mm towards roof; 60mm vertical; 17mm sloping towards floor			14mm sloping towards top; 20mm vertical; 15mm towards floor	76mm (3in) basis		102mm (4in) vertical, 83mm (3.25in) to floor, 51mm (2in) to roof
Hull floor	20mm under driver's compartment; 7mm rearwards	12.7mm mild steel plus 20mm armour (driver's compartment) or 7mm (rearwards)	20mm under driver's compartment; 7mm rearwards	10mm	20mm below driver's compartment; 10mm to 20mm below engine compartment		40mm below turret, 25mm elsewhere,
Hull roof	20mm above driver; 30mm sloping sides of engine compartment; 17mm louvres and covers; 10mm roof elsewhere			10mm	20mm		30mm forward, 25mm above engine compartment
Turret or superstructure front and mantlet	(turret ring only) 65mm	14mm	20mm	(see hull front)	114mm (4.5in) basis		254mm (10in)
Turret sides		14mm	20mm	20mm	102mm (4in) basis		152mm (6in), except 102mm (4in) on box at rear
Turret rear		14mm	14mm	(rear-facing over engine compartment) 20mm	76mm (3in) basis		152mm (6in) vertical, plus 102mm (4in) on bo
Turret roof	(covering turret ring) 9.5mm	8mm	10mm	No roof except two 10mm plates: above gunner; and above driver	20mm		30mm, except 14mm above box

releasing the finger catch underneath. The Triplex block could be removed by releasing a finger catch at bottom left of the shield. Two spare Triplex blocks were carried beside the driver.

The Archer had the same arrangements as the Valentines, except the visor opened upwards, and had no vision slit or look-out block. Some sources have reported incorrectly that the driver was obliged to leave his seat during firing, but the recoil was arrested at 14.5 inches by a hydraulic buffer and two steel

The Valentine III received a larger turret for three men, with a narrower aperture in front of the internal mantlet.

springs, and the driver was needed to realign the vehicle if the target moved outside of the limits of the gun's traverse, to drive the vehicle out of trouble, or to operate the radio in an emergency.

All the proposed Valiants lacked visors, so vision was reduced to two periscopes.

Controls

The driver's feet operated the clutch pedal (leftmost), the auxiliary brake pedal (in the middle) which was rarely needed, and the accelerator pedal (rightmost).

The two levers between his knees acted as steering and braking levers, operating on respective sides. These levers pivoted on a rod attached to a bracket secured to the floor plate, and were connected by rods, turnbuckles and chains to the steering clutch and brake operating gears.

The levers started in the 'hard on' or 'parked' position: pulled back (towards the driver) in order to engage the pawls in the central rack (ratchet). To release the brakes, the driver squeezed together the grips of each lever to withdraw the pawls, flipped over the catch on each lever to hold the grips in the squeezed position, placed his thumbs on top of the catches, and pushed the levers fully forward (engaging the clutches in the final drives). When ready to move, the

This photograph shows the front and nearside of a fully stowed Archer from the first full-production batch. The driver's visor is open. Above him are two periscopes. Below the visor is a length of track. To its nearside is the large container for the coincidence rangefinder, to its offside the 2-inch mortar is stowed. The towing cable is attached on both sides in order to hang below the tow hook. On the front of the trackguard are a fire extinguisher and a jack. The camouflage net is folded atop a stowage bin. The gun is elevated fully, to the same limit as allowed by the Bishop's mounting.

33

The crew of this Valentine I of 20th Armoured Brigade, 6th Armoured Division, in summer 1941, has gathered so much stowage on the engine deck as to obstruct the turret's traverse.

E

1. ARCHER (SP 17-POUNDER), 102ND ANTI-TANK REGIMENT ROYAL ARTILLERY, 15TH (SCOTTISH) DIVISION, IN GERMANY, FEBRUARY 1945

From October 1944, Archers replaced M10 Tank Destroyers in anti-tank battalions of prioritized infantry divisions in Italy and north-west Europe, including 15th (Scottish) Division, which had been a leading 'assault' division since mid-June. It was one of the five 'assault' divisions for the offensive into the Rhineland on 8 February 1945, when it was part of British XXX Corps under 1st Canadian Army, 21st Army Group. On 19 February, during the division's assault on Goch, Churchill tanks supported the infantry during the assault, while the Archers were used to fire indirectly on German positions. After the assault units had captured their objectives, the Archers moved forward to take defensive positions in case of enemy armoured counter-attacks.

This particular vehicle is designated 'L1' as the first gun of 'L' troop, which was usually the self-propelled troop in each battery, while other troops might be using either towed 17-pounders or towed 6-pounders. Each battalion had four batteries, each of three troops. The vehicle designation was sometimes painted below the driver's visor, or on the side towards the gun mounting, but not on this particular vehicle.

2. BISHOP (SP 25-POUNDER GUN), 142ND (ROYAL DEVON YEOMANRY) FIELD REGIMENT (SP) ROYAL ARTILLERY, 1ST CANADIAN INFANTRY DIVISION, IN SICILY, JULY 1943

Bishops were shipped to Egypt over summer 1942, and first used in action in support of the offensive around El Alamein on 23 October 1942. These Bishops were converted to 'Desert Service', just the same as Valentine tanks (see profile A2), except the container for water cans was on the left-hand door at the rear. By the time they reached Tunisia, some users had painted patches of green.

1st Canadian Division deployed to Britain towards the end of 1940. 142nd Field Regiment was one of two British Royal Artillery units assigned to the division. The division enshipped in June 1943 for the Mediterranean, to join XXX Corps (sailing from Egypt, Tunisia and Malta), under 8th Army. The division was one of the seven divisions that landed in Sicily on 10 July, taking the left of the British force, on the right flank of the Americans.

The division's Bishops deployed with an auxiliary fuel tank and water container, but no sandguards or new paint. The turret sides of this battery 'master gun' have been marked in chalk with a code for gun-laying. Field regiments were structured with three batteries, each of eight guns. Bishops remained in service on the Italian mainland throughout most of 1944, until US M7 Priests (SP 105 mm howitzers) and Canadian Sextons (SP 25-pounder guns) equipped all frontline units.

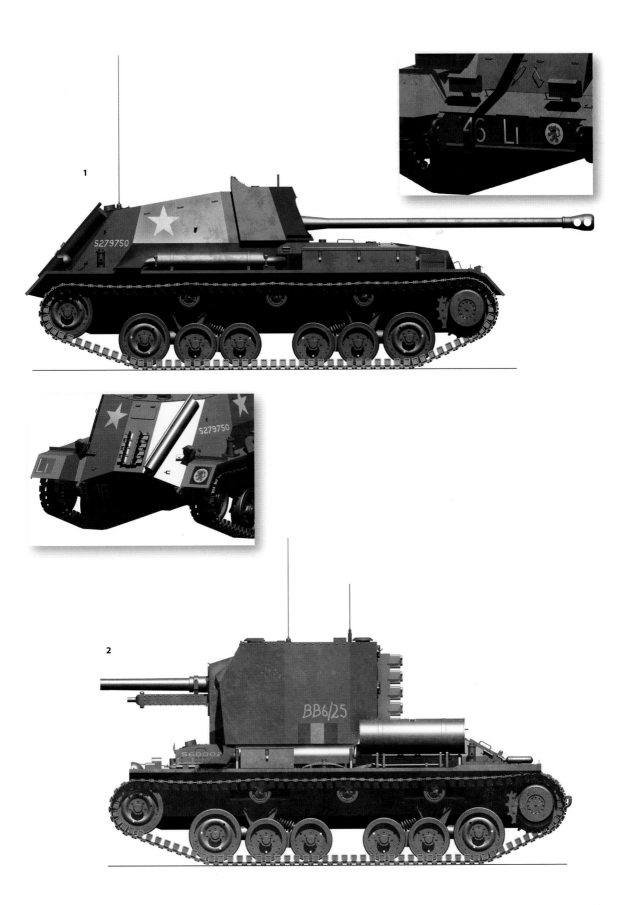

1

S279750

46 L1

L1 46

2

BB6/25

S6000

Archer's roof kit was designed with the gap shortest over the gunner's plate, tallest over the driver's cover plate, and two hatches – here shown open. This kit reached 21st Army Group too late to be installed before the surrender of Germany.

driver depressed the clutch pedal, selected a gear, let out the clutch, and pressed on the accelerator. To steer towards one side, he pulled back the lever on that side. To stop, he pulled back both levers.

The clutch pedal was depressed to release a gear, let out, depressed again to select a gear, and let out again to engage the gear. The gear change lever was located in a gate on the right side of the driver. The lever was connected by universal couplings, selector rods and an adjustable actuating lever to the gearbox. The advance normally started in second gear, with the lever in the middle bottom of the gate. First gear (top right corner) was provided for uphill

The Valentine XI's hull looked the same as the Valentine IX's, with the container for five water cans affixed below the air outlet louvres.

or heavy going. The reverse (bottom right corner) and fifth (top left corner) gears could not be engaged until the driver squeezed a catch on the lever.

Instruments

Forward of the driver, an instrument panel was mounted to the left, a smaller one to the right. The left panel was provided with an ammeter (reading 0 to 60 amps), oil pressure gauge, speedometer, starter button, an ignition switch for the 'flame primer' for cold weather starting, a flame primer hand pump knob, four switches for the exterior lights, a socket for an inspection lamp, and a five-way fuse box. On the Valentine IX, a light switch was added for the convoy lamp, two buttons were added for the tail smoke generators, and a red warning light indicated the master switch was on.

On the right panel was a water temperature gauge, an eight-day clock, and the engine shut-down control, which had three definite positions: if fully out, the fuel injectors and air valve were open; if partially depressed, the fuel injectors were closed but the air valve remained open, as a way to stop the engine normally; if fully depressed, the fuel injectors and air valve were closed, in order to stop the engine in an emergency.

In the Valentine IX, the right panel had only the temperature gauge, a lamp and a lamp switch (off, dim, or bright). The engine shut-down control was a lever to the left of the driver's seat, connected mechanically to the governor; the lever was manipulated forward and down to run the engine, or back and up to stop.

At the rear of the turret, underneath the radio, was another emergency shut-down button.

Electrical power

On the left side hull plate, a master switch was located, which controlled all electrical power in the driving compartment, including the push-button circuit controlling the motor-starting solenoid, but excluding the main current to the starter motor.

If the electrical battery was low, two tanks could be connected to share electrical power via a special cable, stowed on every tank, which could be

On exercise in England in 1941, these Valentine Is and IIs have the curved cover over the exfiltration slit at the rear of the turret, and the centrally located bulbous base for the 6-foot rod aerial used with the Number 11 wireless radio. The Number 19 set was used with a shorter thinner aerial on the offside of the turret roof for higher echelon traffic, and a yet shorter aerial on the nearside for traffic within the troop.

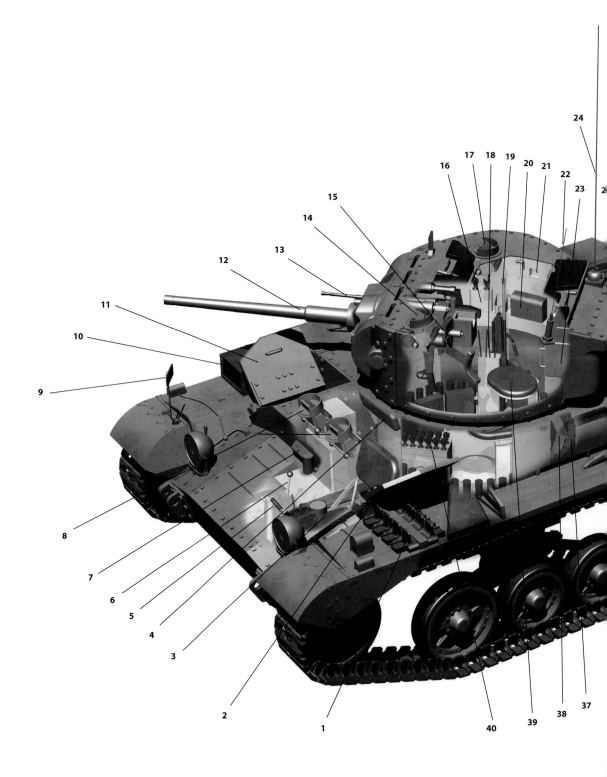

KEY

1. Four track links (spare)
2. Driver's hatch
3. Driver's seat
4. Driver's brow pad
5. Steering levers
6. Gear change lever
7. Driver's visor
8. Driver's periscopes
9. Driving mirror
10. Wood blocks for jack

11. Driver's hatch
12. 40mm 2-pdr gun
13. 7.92mm Besa coaxial machine gun
14. Gunner's rotating periscope
15. Gunner's sighting telescope
16. Two 2in smoke bombs
17. Commander's rotating periscope
18. Four distinguishing flags
19. Bren gun for AA use
20. Signal satchel
21. Commander's 'revolver port'
22. Aerial for Number 24 radio
23. Number 19/24 radio set

24. Aerial for Number 19 radio
25. Stowage bin
26. Air inlet louvres
27. Camouflage net inside tarpaulin
28. GMC 6-cylinder diesel engine
29. Fan
30. Water cans
31. Pyrene fire extinguisher
32. Jack
33. Tow rope
34. Crowbar
35. Shovel
36. Pick head
37. 51 rounds of 2-pdr ammunition around turntable
38. 10 boxes of 7.92mm around turntable
39. Gunner's seat
40. 16 2in smoke bombs

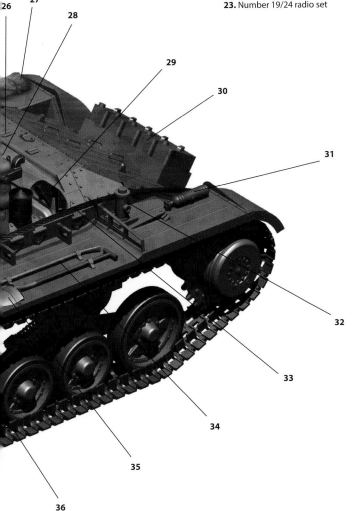

26
27
28
29
30
31
32
33
34
35
36

This is a late-production Archer at Vickers' Elswick Works before completion of its stowage. This vehicle has a tow bar on the rear, as well as the hook at the front.

plugged into the 24-volt socket on the left side of the driver's compartment.

The generator was located on the right side of the engine, supplying electricity through a base junction underneath the turret floor.

Fighting
Vision

In Valentine I, II, IV, VI and VII, the commander was provided with a hatch, a rotating periscope in the hatch, and a large square 'revolver port' in the right side of the turret. Early Valentine Is had three sighting vanes in front of the periscope, whose gaps equated to one degree. All other Valentines had one larger sighting vane. Two spare prisms were stowed – one at the rear, one on the gunner's side.

The gunner looked out via a coaxial sighting telescope or a rotating periscope above, or a D-shaped port to the side (known misleadingly as a 'rear-view look-out'). This look-out was missing from most Valentine Is and some Valentine IIs (tanks numbered T15946 to T16555 and T20419 to T20493).

Since the rear-view look-out lacked splash proofing, bullets impacting around it were likely to find their way inside the turret. Under heavier impact, the parts could fail. In trials, the impact of a 40mm shot dislodged the securing pin of the operating lever on the inside. By the fourth round, the hinge bolts had sheared, and the door had fallen away.

By 1942, MEC was welding shut the ports and look-outs. At home,

This elevated view shows Archer's roof plates and an alternative stowage scheme. Just over the top of the gunner's roof plate can be seen the plate above the driver's position, on top of which the cover for the fighting compartment has been rolled up and secured with straps. On the left is the camouflage net, atop the folded cover for the engine compartment, within which are the blankets. These are strapped atop a bin containing most of the rations, electrical spares, cleaning kits, and other sundries. To the rear of this bin are two wooden blocks for use with the jack, which is obscured by some bundle forward of the silencer. Behind the air outlet louvres are rolled ground sheets. Behind this are the two smoke generators. The track adjusting tool is atop the right-hand bin, which contained most of the tools and spares. A reel of electrical cable has been affixed to the offside of the fighting compartment. On other vehicles it was affixed adjacent on the glacis or the trackguard. This vehicle does not have either a tow hook or a tow bar.

designers replaced them both with a circular revolver port, outside a circular aperture, with a flap that closed down within the bracket. This port was designed into both sides of the turret. This configuration was introduced on the three-man turret, which entered production late in 1941 on Valentine IIIs and Valentine Vs, and continued on the Valentine IX, X and XI, but was forgotten by the designers of the Valiant.

The Valentine IX's commander had a hatch, a rotating periscope in the hatch, a fixed periscope (without any handle) behind the hatch facing rearwards, and a circular revolver port in the right side.

The gunner of the Valentine XI had a small hatch in the leftmost part of the turret roof, a rotating periscope forward of the hatch, and a circular revolver port in the left side of the turret. Two spare prisms were stowed in the turret, as before, except that both were stowed together at the rear of the turret.

Vickers first proposed the Valiant with a single split hatch in the roof of the turret, centrally placed, with a periscope in the roof to the right. The pilot Valiant had a rotating periscope ahead of a split hatch for the commander on the right, and another behind his hatch. Vickers had proposed two periscopes for the gunner, and a large door in the left side of the turret, but the Valiant's had a single rotating periscope forward of his split hatch.

The Bishop's roof had a hatch above the gunner's head, and a visor in the sloping plate, but these were good for little more than ventilation. The commander had a rotating periscope, to the right of the ventilating fan towards the forward edge of the superstructure. The periscope could be locked at any bearing or attainable elevation with two clamping screws. In front of the periscope, a vane sight was mounted on the roof. The gunner's only vision was through a telescopic sight, protruding through a port to the left of the gun. If the sight was too dangerous to use, the port could be closed by a sliding shield on the inside of the superstructure. This shield was secured in the open or closed position by means of a T-handled screw.

In every Valentine, binoculars were stowed above the radio. In the Archer, they were stowed on top of the 2-inch bomb box in the right-hand side of the fighting compartment.

Controls

The gun was elevated via manually operated gears, and traversed via electrically or manually operated gears. For electrical control, the operator engaged the trigger inside the handle, then twisted (pivoted) the handle from vertical (clockwise for rightwards, counterclockwise for leftwards). The powered speed was controlled by the degree to which the control handle was twisted.

The control unit was bracketed to the turret floor in front of the gunner; the electric motor and gearbox were secured to the turret wall in front of the gunner.

Rangefinders

The Archer was designed with stowage for a coincidence rangefinder (Number 2 Mark VII). This could be mounted on a small socket on the upturned plate above the gunner, or on a stand that was normally stowed in the nearside stowage bin. Its container was attached to the left front of the superstructure, which filled with water and ruined the rangefinder. In the short ranges of Normandy and Italy it was reported to be more of an encumbrance, to the extent that users usually left the rangefinders behind in storage.

G   **VALENTINE IIS OF 146TH RAC ATTACK DONBAIK IN BURMA – THE ONLY BRITISH TANK ACTION IN THE FAR EAST IN 1943**

On 1 May 1941, the Indian Army formed the Indian Armoured Corps, and planned to form another seven battalions from cavalry cadres, in order to populate three armoured divisions and one Indian States Forces Brigade by the end of 1942, but Indian units generally received no armoured vehicles until they transferred to Middle East Command.

The British armoured units in India were 3rd Carabiniers, 25th Dragoons and 150th RAC (10th Battalion, York and Lancaster Regiment). These trained with unarmoured vehicles, Bren Gun Carriers and a few Valentines, before receiving US M3 medium tanks late in 1942.

9th Battalion, the Duke of Wellington's Regiment was converted to 146th RAC on 1 November 1941 with three Valentine tanks. It was not fully equipped until November 1942. By the end of 1942, the Japanese had withdrawn from the Indian border to a line from Myohaung through Rathedaung to Donbaik on the coast of the Arakan in north-west Burma. In January 1943, Allied forces sent 14th Indian Division and 146th RAC into the Arakan. 47th Indian Brigade failed to break through the Japanese fortifications at Donbaik on 18 and 19 January. On 1 February 1943, eight Valentine tanks from 'C' Squadron advanced on Donbaik alone, in accordance with 55th Indian Brigade's plan. They turned parallel with the enemy trenches in order to fire into them, but three tanks fell into a ditch, where they were neutralized by enemy infantry. An anti-tank gun disabled a tank from the other troop, after which the four remaining tanks withdrew. Indian infantry then attacked, only to be repulsed. This event persuaded regional commanders to launch no further tank operations in Burma until 1944.

The Valentine XI was the first British tank to be designed with stowage for a rangefinder (Number 12, Mark VIII), but since this was deployed only as a command tank the rangefinders were appropriated for other tanks.

OTHER VARIANTS

The Valentine, due to its availability and reliability, was chosen as a platform for many conversions and experiments, although the larger US M4 Sherman medium tank and Churchill infantry tank superseded it in almost every case.

More variants were converted in the field or tried at home than could be explained in this whole book, but only three conversions were standardized at home: flamethrowers, bridgelayers and mine-clearing flails.

Flamethrower

The Petroleum Warfare Department (PWD) was established on 9 July 1940 to develop flamethrowers to defeat any invaders. In early 1941, a longer-range flamethrower was required for the Churchill tank, and a shorter-range flamethrower for the Valentine. The PWD ordered AEC to install its Heavy Pump Unit in a Valentine I.

The Ministry of Supply's Chief Superintendent Research Department (CSRD) had an Experimental Station at Langhurst, Sussex, which developed its own 'smaller flamethrower', which the Experimental Station at Chertsey, run by Vickers, installed in a Valentine I early in May 1941.

In both cases, the projector was mounted on the offside trackguard, and the fuel was carried in a two-wheeled armoured trailer.

The PWD system developed pressure from compressed hydrogen, whereas the CSRD system developed pressure from slowly burning cordite, which proved spasmodic, so the PWD was preferred, even though it was more difficult to package and protect (due to the large hydrogen bottles). Photographs suggest that the CSRD flame reached targets 60 yards away; the PWD flame reached somewhat further. 12 Valentine IIs and IVs were allocated for conversion to the PWD system, although depot records survive for only two converted Valentine Is (T15998 and T16409); none was deployed, and none survives.

This is the PWD/AEC flamethrower, identifiable by the armoured cover over the projector, the external piping, and the incompletely armoured fuel tank.

In March 1942, Langhurst was transferred to the PWD. Their projects for the 'longer-range flamethrower' were combined as the superior 'Crocodile' system, which was piloted on a Valentine before transfer to the more spacious Churchill.

Bridgelayer

In 1940, the Experimental Bridging Establishment developed the No. 1 scissors bridge, which folded out to 34 feet long and 9.6 feet wide, and was rated for 30-foot (9.1 metre) gaps and loads of 30 imperial tons. The new bridge was tested on a de-turreted Cruiser II, but by September 1941 this platform had been abandoned in favour of the Cruiser V (Covenanter). The bridge was fully developed for the Covenanter, and entered production, before orders were received around January 1942 to redesign the mechanism for the Valentine II.

Mechanism

The mechanism was operated by power taken off the fan drive, through a small oil-bath clutch and a 2-to-1 reduction gear, to a reversing gearbox directly behind the driver, beneath the screw feed gearbox. Deploying and recovering the bridge took 2.5 minutes each.

Use

This was tried on a Valentine I (T16278), with a bridge manufactured in 1941. All subsequent Valentine Bridgelayers used the Valentine II/III platform, since the diesel engine developed more torque to operate the mechanism.

After the pilot conversion, 239 Bridgelayers were produced from January 1943 to August 1944; another 30 spare bridges were ordered in that period.

In January 1943, some Valentine Bridgelayers arrived in Egypt, but without bridges, which had been loaded on to another ship and sent somewhere else. A complete Bridgelayer landed there in March. 25 Bridgelayers were exported to the Soviet Union late in 1943.

Some Valentine Bridgelayers were used in north-west Europe from 1943 to 1945, when the supply of Churchill Bridgelayers could not meet demand, but the Valentine's launching gear was inferior, it lacked the speed to keep up with fighting tanks, its epicyclic steering gave inferior agility to the Churchill's controlled differential, and spares were in short supply.

Each armoured brigade in Italy and India/Burma had six Valentine Bridgelayers. Meanwhile, British forces in India developed a turretless

Bridgelayer '30' is shown without its bridge, revealing the launching mechanism. All these vehicles are serving with 11th Armoured Division in England.

Valentine bridging vehicle nicknamed 'Burmark', with ramps for other vehicles to climb over the hull.

Anti-mine flail

In the field, Valentines were used to push or tow various rollers and ploughs against landmines. From late 1942, MEC was sending glowing reports of its flail ('Scorpion') on Matilda IIs and US M3 mediums. The Scorpion was preferred over the home-developed Matilda 'Baron', whose boom was too wide for landing craft.

The War Office wanted AEC to develop and assemble two ME-pattern Scorpions within two months, towards a requirement for around 500 Scorpions, of which the first 25 kits were to be despatched urgently by air to the western front in Tunisia, for attachment to M3 or M4 medium tanks.

Instead the Ministry of Supply authorized a home-pattern Scorpion, for attachment to a turretless Valentine II, the combination known as UK Scorpion Mark III. On 3 March 1943, the AFV Liaison Meeting (led by the Ministry of Supply, with representatives from the War Office) decided that a contract should be given to AEC.

In April 1943, the Valentine Scorpion started trials at the Obstacle Assault Centre. The pilot was driven over two Tellermines twice without detonating them; on the third run, the flail detonated one of the landmines, which sympathetically detonated the second landmine under the belly of the tank, killing all three crewmen. The next pilot, and subsequent conversions for issue, were given plates of mild steel (0.5 inches thick), with an air space of 2 inches, below the belly.

The flail

The flail utilized 32 chains attached to a drum-like rotor carried in front of the tank by the two side arms. The rotor assembly consisted of a solid drawn steel tube (6.5 inches in diameter at its outsides), stiffened by four quarter angles (2 inches by 2 inches) that were welded to the 32 rotor blades (each 0.5 inches thick), which in turn were welded to the tube. Bolted to the rotor blades were the rotor blade extension pieces, to which the chains were secured by means of a coupling which clamped the last link of the chain and pivoted on a hardened steel brush in the rotor blade extension.

This Scorpion, converted from a Valentine II (T18072), is being used by 79th Armoured Division, early in 1944.

Each chain was about 4 feet 9 inches long, with about 35 links made from steel bars $^9/_{16}$ inches in diameter. It was supposed to be replaced before it was reduced to shorter than 4 feet or 29 links.

Two Ford V8 engines in the main compartment drove the flail via transmissions running inside respective side arms. The engines were governed to a speed of 3,100rpm, at which they developed 80bhp each. The operator was supposed to keep the engines operating at 2,900 to 3,000rpm, so that the flail rotor would revolve at 165 to 170rpm, but they were prone to overheating, despite various attempted solutions. The driver was supposed to advance at up to 1.5mph when flailing mines, 0.75mph against wire.

The turret was replaced by a taller superstructure housing the commander and flail operator. The superstructure was fabricated from flat plates in a complex six-sided plan, with overall dimensions of 8 feet wide, 5 feet long and 3 feet 9 inches tall, and a weight of 1.3 imperial tons. The superstructure was secured to the hull by belting in place of the turret ring.

Access was gained via hinged flaps in the roof. The commander stood on the left, the flail operator on the right, upon a raised platform, above the bevel gearbox. The central part of this platform was hinged to allow access to the driver's compartment.

Use
Twenty-five vehicles were ordered from T.C. Jones & Company of Shepherds Bush, Middlesex. The first entered service in summer 1943. 79th Armoured Division wanted the Scorpions only for training of 30th Armoured Brigade, pending Sherman Crabs. As of 19 February 1944, 118 Scorpion kits had been delivered to Chilwell Depot, which had completed 37 Valentine Scorpions. 21st Army Group had issued 35 vehicles towards a requirement of 90 Scorpions; it took only Sherman Crabs to the continent in June 1944.

FURTHER READING

Ness, Leland S., *Jane's World War II Tanks and Fighting Vehicles: The Complete Guide*, London: Harper Collins, 2002

Perrett, Bryan, *The Valentine in North Africa 1942–43*, London: Ian Allan, 1972

INDEX

References to illustrations are shown in **bold**. Plates are shown with page locators in brackets.